Beyond Green Tea
AND Grapefruit

POEMS AND STORIES

by Gail N. Harada

D1711017

ISBN 978-0-910043-89-2
This is issue #103 (Spring 2013) of *Bamboo Ridge, Journal of Hawai'i Literature and Arts* (ISSN 0733-0308)
Copyright © 2013 by Gail N. Harada

Published by Bamboo Ridge Press
Printed in the United States of America
Indexed in *Humanities International Complete*
Bamboo Ridge Press is a member of the Council of Literary Magazines and Presses (CLMP).

Book Design: Stephanie Chang Design Ink
Cover art: *October* (detail), 2010, by Noe Tanigawa, encaustic, 7" x 11"
Interior art: *Beyond Green Tea* series, 2013, by Noe Tanigawa,
    Lotus #33, #34, #35 & #36, charcoal on vellum, 7" x 7"
Author's photo by Hal Lum

Bamboo Ridge Press is a nonprofit, tax-exempt corporation formed in 1978 to foster the appreciation, understanding, and creation of literary, visual, or performing arts by, for, or about Hawai'i's people. This publication was made possible with support from the National Endowment for the Arts (NEA) and the Hawai'i State Foundation on Culture and the Arts (SFCA), through appropriations from the Legislature of the State of Hawai'i (and grants by the NEA).

Bamboo Ridge is published twice a year. For subscription information, back issues, or a catalog, please contact:

Bamboo Ridge Press
P.O. Box 61781
Honolulu, HI 96839-1781
(808) 626-1481
brinfo@bambooridge.com
www.bambooridge.com

5 4 3 2 1   13 14 15 16 17

for my parents

Saburo & Violet T. Harada

Contents

prologue

A Meditation

A man contemplates the distance
to the horizon from the place he stands
on the reef in the break and surge
of seawater and foam.
He fathoms the near water,
searching through its infinite shifting
for the lightning glimmer of fishscales
or the teal blue turning of an *uhu*
or the fluid shadow of a school of mullet
gliding like one body, quick and elusive,
poised to cast his throw net
into the encroaching twilight tide
on the edge of Waikīkī.
What do the waves tell him?
How does the wind speak?
When does the universe hum inside a man?
A woman listens for something true
in the waves and wind,
trying to discern words which could resonate
in her body and heart, like lines
of an ancient chant, a *mele* moving her
beyond the tranquility of green tea and grapefruit
into a caldera of molten, fearless clarity.

part one

The Fence

at a U.S. Army base, Japan

This is what I remember:
The barbed wire fence
rose along one edge
of the playground
jabbing the blue sky
like the prickly hedge
surrounding Sleeping
Beauty's castle.
It was
the thorniest fence
I'd ever seen.
On my side,
American children
reveled in raucous recess—
playing dodgeball and tag,
chanting singsong
jump rope rhymes.
On the other side
stood a Japanese school
attended by children with
cheeks like cherry blossoms
filling the spring air,
their high-pitched voices
sounding like small bells
or wind chimes
in the distance.
A sandy-haired,
freckle-faced kid
who didn't know

any better
approached and asked,
"Are you Japanese?
Aren't you s'pozed to be there?"
pointing with a pudgy finger
beyond the fence.
I glared at him,
replied, "I'm from Hawai'i,"
and moved closer to
the fence.
On the other side
a Japanese girl
looked at me
and whispered something
into her friend's ear.
They went back
to their game.
I stayed stubbornly
where I was,
extended my right
hand in front of me
and
touched
the fence.

New Year

This is the old way,
the whole clan gathered,
the rice steaming over the charcoal,
the women in the room, talking,
a layer of potato starch on the table.

This is the old way,
the father watching his son lift the mallet,
pound the rice, pound mochi,
the children watching or playing,
the run of the dough to the women,
the rolling of the round cakes.

This is the old way,
eating ozōni, New Year's soup:
mochi for longevity,
daikon, long white radish
rooted firmly like families;
eating burdock, also deeply rooted,
fish for general good luck,
and lotus root, wheel of life.

This is the old way,
setting off firecrackers
to drive away evil spirits,
leaving the driveways red for good fortune.

The new year arrives,
deaf, smelling of gunpowder.

Conversation at Dinner

for my father

You say it's not easy to build a stone wall.
One must decide where to build it,
how tall it should be, its curve,
keeping in mind proportion to the rest of the yard.
There's the clearing, and the carrying of rocks,
the marking with string
for straightness,
and the placing of each rock,
because even stone walls should be built with craft.
Then there's the planting.
You start with healthy shoots,
tend them,
and eventually everything blooms,
the hydrangeas, orchids, birds-of-paradise,
roses, heliconia, anthuriums.
You discipline the yard,
paring the hillside back,
wanting more order, more light.

Grampa

He reminded me of the god of fortune,
fat and smiling, with prosperous earlobes
and an old-timer's plantation pidgin English
peppered with Japanese and Hawaiian,
remnants of his youth in Kahaluʻu
which he didn't pass on to his daughters,
my aunts and my mother,
who spoke proper Standard English.
There's an old photograph of him as a young man
wearing an aviator's helmet
and another of him dressed like a farmer in overalls.
He taught us how to putt golf balls in his living room
and drove a big old white Cadillac with tail fins,
navigating us through Kaimukī
to the old Toho Theatre, now a Papa John's Pizza,
where we watched silly Japanese comedies
inappropriate for children.
I loved the open lanai he built behind his house,
with its clean unpainted wood,
and the place for the *kakemono*.
When I was fifteen he died in his sleep.
That dim early morning, my cousins, my brother, and I
sat silently in the living room
as the policeman and the coroner went about their business
and the adults walked about as if in a fog
until my aunty said,
"Go see Grampa now."
He seemed enormous in his bed,
but he didn't look dead—
he looked like he was sleeping

and might wake up any moment
to take us riding in his big boat of a car.
But he was dead,
the vortex of grief,
as we stood by him, not knowing
what to say or do.
The *bonsan* came on the appointed afternoon
to perform the traditional ceremony,
chanting Buddhist sutras,
punctuating his prayer
by striking a brass bowl that radiated
sound flowing into silence
like a ripple disappears into the surface of water.
We dutifully offered incense.
Later, I went to his bedroom, empty now,
the glare of sunlight on the walls,
the faint essence of incense still in the air.

Grandma's English Lessons

I wonder how Grampa chose my grandmother,
a picture bride, who tried to learn English
from the local Japanese radio station
after he was dead twenty years
and she was in her eighties.
She would point at her knee
and say "nii" triumphantly,
point at her elbow and say "e-rubo,"
proud of her late-blooming English vocabulary.

Chop Suey House Wedding

The whole restaurant is swaying tonight
with the ten-foot surf that's rolling in
from Hurricane Harry.
It's not the whiskey that's making the floor
shift under the tables,
as the dishes clatter and sizzle
good luck and happiness.
The noodles arrive in the midst of speculation
about an appropriate penalty for drunk driving
as everyone toasts to the bride and groom:
Shin-no-shin-pu banzai! Banzai! Banzai!

For My Brother

You tell the story,
how you knew
you had been careless,
not diving into the water
fast enough.
The wave pushed you under
and you felt
your right knee
hit the reef.
You pulled yourself through
to the surface somehow
and made it to shore.

You want to know
how to count the stitches,
those black knots
curved like a centipede
over your patella.
When the doctor
releases your leg,
you take your surfboard and the car,
and head for the sea,
eager to test yourself.

You find the swells
still rise
like glassy walls,
irresistible.
And you catch them,
riding again and again

with a swift balance.
I know what it is like
only near the shore
to stroke and kick like mad
and then,
let the wave transport me
shoreward.

Lono's Place

We pass the guard
his neighbors post outside Haiku Circle.
Today, we are all his guests.
Look, he has raised two Hawaiian flags,
welcoming the people
whose cars line the street.
It's raining,
      a blessing:
      walk barefoot.

We go past the small house,
following path and stream
up the mountainside,
all around the sound of water,
      rain on the thick bamboo,
      ripe guavas,
      rain beading on the taro leaves.

We reach the waterfall's
      sheer cliff
           and pool.
People perch on rocks,
and a few wade into the shallow pool
to touch the clear ribbon of water.

Returning, we come upon
      a smaller fall
           and deeper pool.
One by one we slip
into the water,

going under, coming up,
        our clothes heavy and darkened.

The way back needs so few words.

On the Edge of the Island

The water recedes,
leaving white veins that trickle away
down the crevices of rocks
which once seared their way
toward the ocean.
There is a dark stain on this ledge.
Torn seaweed rises and falls
with the crescendo
and decrescendo of the waves.
The salt wind gusts hard,
relentless against the slopes
and the scrawny scrub trees
that stubbornly endure.

See how the colors retreat,
like the rare birds,
'i'iwi, 'ākepa.

Pomegranate

Even now she sometimes
thinks of the child
she might have had.
The woman had been kind,
chanting Hawaiian over the boiled pomegranates
night after night.
The hot brew stank,
made the girl nauseous.
The boiled fruit were soft,
brown, bitter.
Later, curious, she tried a fresh pomegranate.
She sliced through the leathery skin
to the chambers of red seeds,
each seed a jewel, a fish egg
tipped with blood.
She ate it deliberately,
pulling seed from skin,
staining her fingers with the sweet juice.

Animus

I rise from his luminous bed
three times,
three times dreaming of dark rooms.

Once I rise alone
in a house
which smells of damp earth and old furniture.
Alone, I wander through the silent rooms.

I rise again,
a branch of tender shoots,
a whole fresh fig.
I am the full moon
passing through a sky of dark rooms.

The dark-haired man smiles in his sleep.
He glows, so full of light!
Inside
all the doors open.
Antique chests unlock.
Orchids bloom wildly in the corners of the rooms.

I rise once again.
My hands gesture slowly
the way his hands move when he speaks.
I feel myself turn slowly
into the man who sleeps in his own light
in a room behind me.

Hearing a Train Whistle at Night

How long it is,
thinning,
a little sad,
like a graying late afternoon.
It makes me think of distance,
almost interminable,
a few scattered lights in the flat blackness.
The slow thundering is almost interminable too,
and it seems the train itself must stretch a mile
as it rumbles past.
It becomes quiet,
only the sound of the clock ticking,
the dripping faucet.
It's strange to think of so much land,
like trying to think of the whole Pacific Ocean.
I owe letters.
It is getting late.

First Winter

We are far from what held us then.
You will not live again in that house
where you could hear footsteps
shuffling through the long ironwood needles,
and there are houses to which I will not return.

Now you send letters about your new life,
but sometimes there is that reflection back.
You write "The spy life is over,"
we are young girls no longer.
The language you are learning
is melodious and quick.
You say you are beginning to dream in it.
You tell me of islands lovelier than any vision,
and of three bays:
Anse Vata, Baie des Citrons, Baie de l'Orphelinat.

I will tell you of the river at night
and what it is to want to walk closer to its edge.
I will tell you of the snow which turns one back
into the curve of the body,
that quiet and its steady falling
which keeps me by the window for hours,
of a silence those ironwoods
never gave, not even after a light rain.

7 O'Clock

He wakes me up
long distance.
There it is two in the morning
and he has just gotten home from work.
Here the mist rises from the river.
The yellow tree by my window
almost fools me into thinking
the sun is shining.
Where he is,
it is dark,
the crests of waves advance white
in the moonlight,
and the ocean is blacker
than any river.
But he doesn't think about the ocean,
his voice reaching through the telephone lines,
trying to touch me.
Suddenly my desires become simple.

Bellows Field, End of Summer

The colors of the sky and sea muted,
the waves subsided
as the afternoon approached the color of ironwood.

The waves lapped my feet as I strolled,
each step a soft sinking
near the mild splashings of children.

I wasn't prepared to see
the man floating face down
so close to shore in the grey green water.

"Billleeee!"
A young man hurtled through the shallow water,
scooped up the limp body and carried it ashore.

"Somebody call 911!"

The drowned man looked like a young GI,
crewcut, skin stretched taut over his temples.
He was a delicate blue, like a fetus,
like the Portuguese man-of-wars
the currents and winds bring sometimes.

A crowd gathered.
The ambulance arrived
and departed, sirens wailing.

Wherever he went,
I hope he came back

and did not go with death,
the cold night rain leaving
the sand pocked and erased of everything.

Seasons of an Island Life

One almost forgets how time passes
living in such a tropical place.
Summer seems eternal.
I mark the seasons by
the blooming of plumeria or ginger,
the ripening of mangoes or lychee,
the time the sun rises and sets.

It is different from the ordered cycles
of four and a half years
of childhood in Japan.
There each season was distinct:
in the warmth of spring, flurries of cherry blossoms;
in the humidity of summer, ripe watermelons and peaches;
in the briskness of autumn, delicate-leafed red *momiji*;
in the chill of late winter, plum blossoms in the snow.

The buildings here rise
closer and higher.
Over the years
it becomes difficult to recall
the landscape without them.

How clear childhood seems
in spite of everything,
filled with promise,
each season a temperament, predictable.
The long summer has its passages.
I grow older, wanting
the vivid flower, perfect fruit
no matter what the season.

Painted Passages

I.
The even weave of the canvas
becomes as familiar
as childhood, perhaps
an expanse of sky or sea,
the ground we walk on barefoot,
and the task at hand seems clear.
It is what we wish for
secretly,
like a craving for tamarinds
or shave ice,
or the taste of salt
water.
It is a beginning.
Rain.
A spring that flows
into a pond,
a stream,
the sea.
The frame must be perfectly
true.
Push its corners into a door.
Measure it with steel tape.
Stretch the canvas over the frame
and the instinct of experience
takes over.
Pull the canvas.
Feel the taut
surface
tight and even.

A drum to beat out soundless rhythm.
Prepare the canvas to receive color.
Size it with something supple enough,
rabbit or calfskin glue.
Prime it
with an unbelievable whiteness—
No-snow, no-cloud, no color.
This is the whiteness of light,
of sleep,
of the space behind human eyes.
This is the rhythm of labor,
of sweat.
The hands and fingertips remember its feel
like a prodigal remembers a house,
a room,
the given colors of a landscape.

II.
Your mother wants you
to come home,
and keeps telling me so,
believing in the persuasive powers
of friendship.
She's afraid for you,
living on the edge
in what she thinks is the crime capital
of the universe,
where, according to Charles Osgood,
dog bites are down
and human bites are up 23% this year.

But your letters are filled only
with the excitement of living
in a city that never sleeps,
with the heady whirl

of art openings, galleries,
and the most incredible people—
people who remind one not so much of jewels,
as they do of brilliant neon lights
that stun you with their electricity.

Come to New York and be famous,
you tell me.
Opportunity is just waiting to be picked
like a ripe purple plum
in the Big Apple, you say,
trying to persuade me
across an entire ocean and continent
again.
And sometimes those bright lights you thrive on
almost feel like the sun
to me. Almost.

What can I say to explain this
or any other choice?
When I was on the mainland,
the torpor of winter
kept depositing itself
on my tropic bones,
making me long
for the blue Pacific Ocean,
the ripeness of mangoes,
crests of waves in moonlight,
the myriad greens of the Ko'olau,
and this island that shudders
under the growing weight of its concrete,
waiting.

I try to shape all these colors,
define or obliterate them

with black or white.
What pulls me here is not nostalgia,
but a conviction
deeper than blood.

III.
Just a few strokes
of inspiration,
a little light
to fly towards,
is all I ask.

What consumes me
is rain in the morning,
the daily bowl of rice,
the small everyday tasks,
and some passage
to another side
of home.

Infinity in the Space Between

in memory of Wayne Kaumualii Westlake

It was on-the-job training for Poets-in-the-Schools—
tag along and watch a poet teach for a day.
I tagged along, and
the next night he stopped by
to drop something off.
I don't know what made him stay until 1 a.m.
just talking.
Maybe my books looked like friends—
the *Tao Te Ching*, Mao's *Little Red Book*,
Nānā I Ke Kumu, Fornander's *Hawaiian Antiquities*,
stacks of contemporary American poets,
poetry in translation.
I don't know why he decided to tell me
about Vietnam.
A conscientious objector was not spared
the sight of a man's intestines strung
like Christmas lights
in the branches of a tree,
had to witness a friend
accused of being Viet Cong
pushed from a helicopter,
couldn't stop what was happening,
still sees the look on his friend's face
in those last moments.
His eyes seemed to gaze into the still present past.
As he talked, the room filled
with the news images of that time—
the anti-war protests, the famous war photos,
the napalm girl,

the point-blank execution of a Viet Cong guerilla.
"Look at this."
He pulled out his driver's license.
The state pretends it can prove his identity
but this piece of plastic, these numbers
are not who he is,
these numbers are irrelevant to Hawaiian identity.
I listened. He talked until he felt he was done.
We never spoke of these things again.
He published some of my poems
in one of the anthologies he edited.
Sometime later he moved to the Big Island.
I finished the second part of a PITS residency
he had started at Olomana Youth Correctional Facility.
A few years passed
and he appeared in a dream.
Shadowy figures carrying torches
circled the rim of Kīlauea crater.
Darkness was edged with light from their fire
and the glow of lava in the distance.
It was silent and he was there.
He had never appeared in a dream before
so I was surprised but not disturbed
until a few days later when I turned a page
in *The Honolulu Star-Bulletin*
and saw his obituary—
"Services for Isle Activist Slated at Volcano Crater."
He had died two weeks after a two-car collision.
Police had opened a negligent homicide investigation.
Those closest to him were preparing for a funeral ceremony
"believed to be without precedent . . . .
with Hawaiian kupuna, or elders, selecting the best day."
The light in the room seemed suddenly surreal,
the ground shifted.
The Western world had no answers.

part two

Witness the Lotus

Witness the lotus
how it grows in the mucky sludge
its edible root when cut crosswise
a wheel of fortune
mired in the dark pond bottom
obscured by murky waters.

See how the slender green snake
of its stem lifts out of the water
above the floppy leaves
transforms from shoot
to bud
to blossom
translucent shell
petals cradling light
opening outward
further out of flower
center hardening
into a pod holding small
seed eyes turned skyward
until they fall out
and sink through the cool murky water
back into that soft mucky sludge.

Somewhere in This World

Somewhere in this world
anything is possible.

ʻŌhiʻa lehua might take root in black lava
or high on a windy cliff
with blossoms beautiful as the perfect velvet-red rose.

New leaves after devastation
might emerge thicker and more verdant than before.

A native hibiscus, *kokiʻo keʻokeʻo*,
growing in a schoolyard
might unfurl its delicately fragrant petals
one ordinary morning as traffic merges on the freeway.

A mountain might stand more majestic
Adorned again with stories told in the reborn air.

Letter to Paris

Old letters accumulate like dust on my desk.
Yours arrive decorated with stamps
from another country.
Across the valley the dogs are at it again,
passing their messages along Pālolo Avenue,
following the musical ice cream truck.
The ants keep crawling out of their holes,
anti-Semitic Frenchmen paint swastikas
on the Jewish confectioner's shop
on your street,
and the years keep slipping by.
Ten, twenty, thirty...
the years fall behind us
like crumbs in some dark forest.
You write of our lives
half over, lost, stewing in some witch's iron pot.
I want to deny it,
but the unwritten poems remain silent and dark,
and less is accomplished than imagined.
We blame the daily business of living
that's consuming our adult lives,
termites eating away at our dreams—
the cooking, the cleaning, the laundry
that never fails to overflow the hamper,
the chores that wait like beasts with feral eyes.
I remember a mutual friend's plaintive refrain:
"There must be more to this life!"
and I believe there is.
You have a daughter with dark hair and a gypsy name,
and I just know that she must be beautiful.

If Dogs Were Men

My friend is upset at her husband
who is her husband legally
but not truly.
She's the one having the scandalous affair,
but she's mad because she's piecing together
the jigsaw of her marriage
and seeing for the first time
irrefutable evidence of his infidelities
committed long before she even considered hers.
"Men are dogs!" she yells into the phone.
"Wait a minute," I say, looking at Ricky,
my large handsome part Lab,
part pit bull, maybe part pointer poi dog
found at Hale'iwa Beach Park
with his left hind leg broken in three places,
who had to go to two sessions of obedience school
before he barely passed,
who adopted Olivia the orphan cat
and became her knight in black fur,
protecting her from the meanest cat gang in Liliha,
who is gentle with Pootie my orange tabby,
and diplomatic with Oscar the bully cat,
"You're complimenting men."
My friend laughs, "Oh yeah, I forgot about Ricky."
Ricky dozes on the kitchen floor,
and his right ear twitches as if he heard his name.
Some nights I can hear the rhythm
of his breathing and low snore
all the way from the kitchen to the bedroom.
"Who's that?" my friend demands.

"Do you have a man in the house?"
"No, it's just Ricky snoring," I explain.
"He sounds like a man!" she exclaims.
"He's trying to turn into a man just for you!"

What if Ricky were a man?
"He'd be fit," my friend speculates,
"but not obsessed with his body.
He'd be strong, but sensitive."
She exhales a dreamy sentimental sigh.
"He'd be devoted to you," she fantasizes.
"But not suffocating," I add.
"He'd be macho," she asserts.
"But not too samurai," I qualify.
She turns pragmatic. "He'd know
how to fix things around the house."
"Could he cook?" I ask.
She pauses. "I don't think so.
But he'd appreciate everything you cooked."
"He'd love animals and children," I declare.
She goes on, "He'd be faithful.
He'd have integrity."
Her voice rises in pitch.
"He wouldn't be a lying,
cheating, two-timing,
hypocritical amoeba!
He'd try to evolve.
He'd do more than just tell interesting stories.
He'd communicate!"
The telephone lines buzz fury across a continent and ocean.
"You could have an intelligent conversation with him!
Do you know what it's like
to live with a man for twenty years
and never have a real conversation?"
I can imagine.

Ricky wakes up, stretches his sturdy body,
ambles over, rests his chin on my knee,
and gazes at me with his big brown doggy eyes.
"He'd be a real sweetie," my friend sighs.
"He already is," I reply.

The Kiss

What longing is revealed by the tilt of the woman's head
and the pale edge of her jaw?
What mystery in the tender shadows of the man's face?
The curve of her hair swoons against her neck.
Is her heart in her throat?
If her heart were a lake,
would their kiss send a shaft of ineluctable light
plunging into the depths?
If his heart were a lake,
would their kiss summon a prehistoric fish
to rise up, glance the moon-dappled surface,
and journey toward primal headwaters,
toward the knowledge they both desire?

A Local Man's Work

Few outside the trade see
the oil refinery in shutdown
the crew pulling the 12-hour night shift
there on the 'Ewa plain
where the effluent flame
of a flare stack burns night and day
and the relentless hiss and clang of industry
can drain a man's spirit if he lets it
30 miles from the reefs off Waikīkī
where he knows traveling mullet play
shadows on their ancient journey
between Lā'ie and Pearl Harbor.

Few outside the trade know
how a man keeps his hood
pulled down deliberately
shutting out everything
except the arc of his torch
its blinding heat
the sparks that singe
smoke that stings
as he welds metal to metal
in a tank or vessel or pipe
his exits blocked
focusing on the work at hand.

Few outside the trade comprehend
the uncertainty of work
the slippery edge between safety and disaster
the hard labor of forcing and being forced

by inorganic metals and equipment
to do the job
how so much depends on the weld
that it withstand the scrutiny of X-rays
that it withstand the pressure
of 22,000 pounds of catalyst per minute
1200 degrees Fahrenheit shooting through
like the pyroclastic flow of a volcanic explosion.

Few witness the sun rising
over the barren expanse
of a dirt parking lot
near 5:40 in the morning
turning a blanket of clouds above Kapolei
a transitory pale gold spun honey
against the incandescent azure sky.
Few see no matter how bone-tired a man emerges
the shadow of exhaustion in his eyes
the gritty residue of grime and sweat on his skin
how he goes forward from his night's labor
into the uncompromising unadulterated light of day.

Journeys to the Horizon

Once upon a time
there was a man or a woman
and he/she lived happily enough
but not ever after.
The inevitable came sooner
rather than later.
The news of its impending
mystery was unexpected,
a sudden rainstorm
on a day when
the sky appeared
so clear and so blue,
the horizon so distant.

Once upon a time
there was a man or a woman
who embarked through unfamiliar territory
toward a horizon
which had become more tangible.
The rain falls,
leaves shimmer
green in the wind,
the streams flow swift and cool
over round stones,
plummet down island cliffs,
go underground
through blind caverns,
emerge in light,
merge with the salt
of the ocean.

Once upon a time
there was a community
which gathered
around a man or a woman
on his/her journey
to a horizon that appeared
to be a line,
a boundary,
the edge of the earth.
The community went
as far as it could
and turned a burden
into a gift.

Once upon a time
there was a man or a woman
who journeyed
toward a horizon
and became something
other and wonderful,
still part of the earth,
still one with the ʻāina,
an ʻōlapa tree
shimmering light
green leaves
in the breeze.

Once upon a time
and forever,
a man and a woman
journeyed toward a horizon
and saw it was a mirror—
sun/moon
day/night
life/death.

The new moon rose,
barely visible
but there,
surrounded by stars.
The man and the woman danced,
touched by a poignant sweetness
born of pain and grief and
love.

A Question

I learned the vocabulary of cancer
to comprehend the cancers of others;
then it disrupted my own life—
the biopsy results of the "suspicious abnormality"
arrived the day after Thanksgiving 2004.
The news was not good:
There was a war in Iraq,
trouble everywhere,
and I had cancer.
It didn't make sense,
the network news coverage,
the phone call from the doctor,
all sounds dissolving into white noise,
words being scribbled on sheets of paper
whirling beyond my grasp.

I learned the terminology of pathology—
Invasive Ductile Carcinoma, Grade III, Stage I,
Estrogen Receptor Negative,
HER2 Negative—
the most significant of 30-plus factors
measured and assayed after the lumpectomy
and sentinel lymph node biopsy.

I was drafted into the war on cancer.
The next assault was High Dose Radiation therapy
twice a day for five days,
each session concluding with the technician
scanning my body with the Geiger counter,
cheerful banter with the radiologist and nurse.

Then I learned the uncomfortable details of chemotherapy
and the language of cancer insinuated itself into each day,
echoing the words of war—
"fight," "battle," "destroy," "kill"—
resembling the jargon of war
in technical specificity and distance—
"prognostic significance" is "unfavorable."
Numbers became critical code about blood and body;
medical terms and pharmaceutical names became
familiar as the weather—neutropenia, Adriamycin, Cytoxan.
Zofran, Ativan, Compazine, Neulasta.
The acronyms of the Iraq war—
WMD—Weapons of Mass Destruction,
IED—Improvised Explosive Device—drifted through
the haze between the chemo treatments,
floated in the alphabet soup of cancer—
RBC—Red Blood Cells,
WBC—White Blood Cells,
ANC—Absolute Neutrophil Count.

War was being waged against cancer in my body
and a war was being fought far away on foreign soil
charted by numbers
coded by acronyms.
The October 26, 2005 *New York Times* noted
a milestone—officially 2,000 American dead,
unofficially an estimated 30,051 Iraqi dead—
witness to what we only glimpsed on television,
the grim events of war—
the daily numbers of deaths, locations, causes—
documented by a timeline that resembled a hospital monitor screen
dotted with tiny maps multiplying like small tumors on the page.

War is cancer and cancer is war:
When and how will it end?

Sky Watching

It was many years ago that a father took his two children up Tantalus to witness Ikeya-Seki's huge comet tail sweep the eastern sky. They were impressed by this astronomical phenomenon and did not comprehend its impact on them. Later, occasional shooting stars flashed through their lives—fleeting, unarticulated wishes waiting to be fulfilled nevertheless. When Halley's comet re-entered Earth's orbit, the angle of its path to that of Earth's diminished its tail to human eyes, so it seemed small compared to the clouds of galaxies and rivers of stars stretched across the black dome of sky above the obsidian expanse of Kīlauea crater. The configuration of Venus, Mars, and Jupiter clustered beside a sliver of crescent moon one June night in 1991 inspired curiosity and anticipation, but *The Honolulu Star-Bulletin* declared the grouping had "little scientific significance." In July of the same year, solar eclipse devotees from around the world descended on the Big Island, only to be foiled by cloud cover that parted for just a few moments during the four minutes of totality. At the same time in a parking lot near Diamond Head, a community gathered, straining to see the moon's penumbra on the sun through special optical grade solar filters. The birds grew quiet, a dusk that never deepened into night settled and lifted, and life went on. In the spring of 1993, the Perseid meteor shower raised spectacular expectations—visions of hundreds of falling stars streaking the night sky. The predictions were not fulfilled, though the faithful who kept watch claimed they were not entirely disappointed. Then, late one November evening as the moon emerged from its eclipse encircled by a faint lunar rainbow, like the princess of clouds and mist on the seventh day of the seventh month in the old Japanese folk tale, a woman began crossing over the Milky Way toward a mystery that could not be denied, a memory that could not be forgotten, and an unexpected path.

The Story the RCA Man Told
While Fixing the Telex
Machine

Once, in Italy, during World War II,
he dreamt his brother had been killed,
a dream so tangible
he knew it had to be reality.
They were both in the 442
but in different companies
somewhere in Italy—
somewhere among the bitter olive trees,
somewhere among the ruined vineyards,
somewhere hidden in the ambivalent golden hills,
somewhere near blood oranges so vivid
he still remembers their fragrance and taste
even after all these years.
Somehow he got permission to go to Headquarters
to look for his brother among the dead soldiers,
side by side, row after row,
decomposing beneath dark woolen blankets
which felt rough and itchy to him
as he lifted up their corners gingerly,
afraid to see but compelled to look
closely at each human face.
Quietly, faraway, matter-of-factly, he says,
"Dead people smell terrible, you know.
But it's the funniest thing," he pauses.
"Up close they smell like celery.
Really, you know—celery."
He didn't find his brother there;

they both survived and came home.
But to this day, when he walks
past the iceberg lettuce and romaine,
past the cucumbers and watercress
freshly spritzed and glistening
at Star Market or Times,
the pale green vegetable odor of celery
swells in the controlled supermarket air
and reminds him of death's harvest
under those somber blankets in Italy.
So he never buys celery,
never thinks of it as light or fresh,
but he says he'll eat it
if it would be rude
or otherwise impossible to refuse.

The Legacy

It's the beginning of rush hour
on Kapiʻolani Boulevard
in front of the Blue Dolfin Lounge
across Cutter Chevrolet
on Friday the 13th
when the front of my car explodes
and smoke or maybe steam
pours out from under the hood.
The service station guy I call sends a tow truck
but I can hear in his voice
that he's thinking:
What's dis wahine talking about—exploded?
Probably jes' one hose pulled out.
Exploded? Nah. She jes' exaggerating.
The next day he calls and says
"Sonofagun, it really was one explosion!
Get one big hole in da radiator.
One big chunk got blown out.
Never seen anything like it before. Sonofagun."

So I think, is it a sign?
A message from my father
via his silver Subaru Legacy?
I feel moderately guilty
even though I did change the timing belt
and I did have the CV boots replaced
and I do take it once a month to full serve.
This time it's going to be expensive.
This time it's going to cost big bucks.
The service station guy points out

"Still cheaper than buying one new car."
My anxious friends say
"Better to be safe. New cars are more reliable."
The service station guy says
"New cars break down all da time."
My friends say
"What kind of car would you get?
The Toyota Echo is cute.
You don't have to haggle for a Saturn."
But I think of the fact that my father's car
is a Subaru Legacy. A Legacy.
The name reverberates with meaning.
Did the Legacy blow up because of something I'm failing to do?
Is this some kind of car *bachi*—an admonition?
Or is it a sign that I need to let the car go?

My father's silver Legacy is pragmatic,
with reinforced side doors
and solid engineering,
the car my father took fishing,
that he could load a kayak onto,
stick a cooler into,
haul fish and *tako* home in.
When he went places with my mother
they used her sleeker Camry instead.

After my father passed away,
we found his Legacy didn't have much resale value,
so I sold my car and adopted his.
"It doesn't match you," my mother said,
turning her critical eye on me as I fastened my seatbelt,
ready to drive the Legacy away from her house.
"It's not feminine and it's not a very nice color."
"A car is not a fashion accessory," I replied,
sliding the key into the ignition.

It takes a month to fix the car this time.
The mechanic replaces the damaged radiator,
thermostat, upper hose, lower hose,
bypass hose, transmission cooler hoses,
hose clamps, gaskets, P.C.V. valve,
ignition wire set, and spark plugs,
and while testing the car, discovers
what caused the explosion—
both radiator fans are broken.
The dealer has only one fan in stock
for a 12-year-old Subaru Legacy
and special orders another fan
which takes 21 days to arrive
from Japan via California.
Is this a sign? A warning?
Let go the car or keep fixing it?
Is it a message from my father?

What would he say?

He would say
"It's just a car."

Finding My Father in Bruyères

MY FATHER WENT TO BRUYÈRES TWO TIMES in his life—in 1944, when he was sent there during World War II, and in 1994 when he and my mother went on the 442nd Regimental Combat Team's reunion tour to re-visit the places the veterans had been during the war and to commemorate the 50th anniversary of the liberation of Bruyères and the rescue of the Lost Battalion. Both times, my father was there in October, in the fall. I traveled to Bruyères in the spring, in April 2009, a year after my mother's passing and twelve years after my father died.

It was my first trip to Europe, with a friend I had known since high school who had lived in Paris for six years after she got married. We took the train from Paris to Strasbourg at dawn. We were to meet her friends, Jean-Pierre and Chantal Kaspar, who now lived in the Vosges but had never been to Bruyères. They were kind enough to offer us a place to stay and to drive us there the next day. I gazed out the train window at the landscape enveloped by the thick morning fog. Until the fog burned off, the sun was just a ghostly presence above the ethereal trees. It felt almost as if the train was taking me to another world. I thought of my father, of how little he had said about the war. He mentioned having tasted blood oranges in Italy. He mentioned that the forests near Bruyères were freezing cold and that once he was in a foxhole and peered over the top at the exact moment a young German soldier in another foxhole was doing the same thing. My father ducked down and popped back up ready to fire, but the young German soldier was gone. He told me how once he and his fellow soldiers were so elated to find a barn to spend the night that they stupidly lit a fire and could have been killed by Germans. He said he was called "Annamite!" by children who thought he and the other 442nd soldiers were Vietnamese. I wondered what he thought on his 1994 tour retracing the 442nd's wartime journey, seeing the peaceful countryside, the bustling towns, the tranquil forests. He didn't divulge much about the friends he lost or about what he actually did during the war. I didn't even know what company he was with; all I knew was that he had served in the 442nd, one of the most decorated combat units in U.S. military history.

We met Jean-Pierre and Chantal in Strasbourg and visited the medieval town of Obernai on the way to their home. After Obernai, we passed picturesque village houses with red tiled roofs, sighted two storks tending to their nest atop a house, drove by acres of vineyards, and admired the gently rolling French countryside framed by the mountains in the distance. The mirabelle plum trees were blossoming in their town.

The next morning, we drove to Bruyères. The sky was blue, the trees were green, spring was in bloom—so different, I think, from what my father must have seen the first time on his way to Bruyères that cold October in 1944.

Before I left on my trip to France, I had met Pierre Moulin, the author of *U.S. Samuraïs in Bruyères*, at the recommendation of Ted Tsukiyama, a veteran who is my friend Fuku's husband. Mr. Moulin knew people in Bruyères who could show me where the 442nd had been. He told me I should meet Bernard Hans and André Freminet, who knew all about the Chemin de la Paix et de la Liberté (the Peace and Freedom Trail) and the historical monuments commemorating the 442nd Regimental Combat Team's liberation of Bruyères and the rescue of the Lost Battalion. He was very helpful and gave me the name of someone he knew who worked for the Hôtel de Ville (City Hall) and could take care of arranging my meeting Monsieur Hans and Monsieur Freminet. Mr. Moulin told me she was going to be on holiday when I would be visiting Bruyères but would tell one of her co-workers about the arrangements she was making for me. I was expected to go to the Hôtel de Ville at 9:00 a.m., Wednesday, April 15.

We arrived a little before 9:00 a.m. on the steps of the Hôtel de Ville. The first thing we saw inside was a glass case displaying memorabilia commemorating various anniversary visits by veterans, including a U.S. army uniform, two koa wood poi pounders, a red flag signed by members of the Texas Lost Battalion, some issues of *The Honolulu Advertiser* and *The Garden Isle*, military medals, and photographs. When we arrived, we discovered that no one had been informed that we would be coming. There had apparently been some mix-up in communication. The adjutant mayor, Monsieur Michaud, was most gracious and helpful, and went back into his office to make some phone calls to see if he could find Monsieur Hans or Monsieur Freminet. While we were waiting in the lobby, a stocky older gentleman with a weathered, pleasant face came into the lobby and asked who was from Hawai'i. He said in French that he had heard that a child of the 442nd was at the Hôtel de Ville and that he had come to see who I was. It felt funny to be called a child of the 442nd. I suppose the village is quite small, and word travels quickly. The man said that when he was nineteen, he was one of the village guides who took small groups of 442nd soldiers up into the mountains where the Lost Battalion was trapped. The forests were full of Germans and the terrain was difficult. The Vosges campaign, which included the liberation of Bruyères and the rescue of 211 soldiers of the Lost Battalion, exacted a heavy toll: 216 Nisei soldiers were killed and 856 were wounded. There were more dead and wounded than those still able to fight. The man told me his name and gave me his card—Edouard Canonica. He wanted to know my father's name. I told him it was Saburo Harada and that my father had come to Bruyères in 1994 for the 50th anniversary of the rescue of the Lost Battalion. Monsieur Canonica said that he also attended the 50th anniversary celebration and had looked for veterans he thought had been in the groups that he had guided into the forest where the Lost Battalion was trapped. He had gotten some of their signatures, but he said he was old and couldn't remember names so well. He lived just ten minutes away from the Hôtel de Ville and would go home and get his book with the signatures. He rushed off and came back a little while later with an old hardcover book, *Americans: The Story of the 442d Combat Team* by Orville C. Shirey, which I was surprised to see had been published in 1946 by the Infantry Journal Press. (Shirey used the military spelling *442d* in the book title.) Monsieur Canonica asked me if I knew what company my father had been with, but I didn't, so he directed me to just turn to the appendix where the names of all the 442nd soldiers were listed. I turned the first few pages of listings, and then, on the fourth page, in the Antitank Company section, I saw my father's familiar signature in the left margin next to "Pfc Saburo Harada, BSA, CIB, GB." I couldn't stop tears from welling up and the page blurred—my father had signed Monsieur Canonica's book twelve years before; my father had been a young soldier here sixty-five years ago. Seeing my father's signature, the physical manifestation of his presence, was overwhelming. "Elle est trés ému," my friend said softly to her friends in the hushed lobby— *she is very moved.* If all the arrangements had gone as planned, I would have never met Monsieur Canonica, and I would have never seen my father's signature in his book. It was such an incredible coincidence that it felt as if it was meant to happen, and I still struggle to find the words to express what I felt then—a sense of wonder and amazement perhaps, maybe a sense of the mystery of life, and perhaps most deeply, gratitude for the

Photo of my father when he was young

unexpected gift of finding a tangible sign of my father instead of having just an abstract awareness that he had been there.

The adjutant mayor returned to the lobby to tell us that he had found Monsieur Freminet, who was on his way. He had also contacted the superintendent of the Épinal Memorial Cemetery, who was an American and wanted to speak with me. On the phone, the cemetery superintendent told me that another descendant of a 442nd veteran was coming to Épinal at 2:00

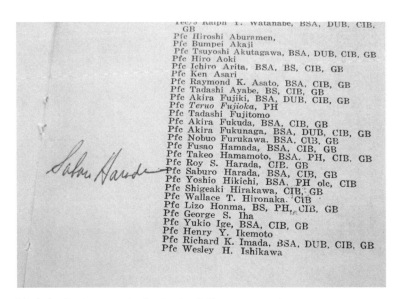

Tec/5 Ralph T. Watanabe, BSA, DUB, CIB,
GB
Pfc Hiroshi Aburamen,
Pfc Bumpei Akaji
Pfc Tsuyoshi Akutagawa, BSA, DUB, CIB, GB
Pfc Hiro Aoki
Pfc Ichiro Arita, BSA, BS, CIB, GB
Pfc Ken Asari
Pfc Raymond K. Asato, BSA, CIB, GB
Pfc Tadashi Ayabe, BS, CIB, GB
Pfc Akira Fujiki, BSA, DUB, CIB, GB
Pfc Teruo Fujioka, PH
Pfc Tadashi Fujitomo
Pfc Akira Fukuda, BSA, CIB, GB
Pfc Akira Fukunaga, BSA, DUB, CIB, GB
Pfc Nobuo Furukawa, BSA, CIB, GB
Pfc Fusao Hamada, BSA, CIB, GB
Pfc Takeo Hamamoto, BSA, PH, CIB, GB
Pfc Roy S. Harada, CIB, GB
Pfc Saburo Harada, BSA, CIB, GB
Pfc Yoshio Hikichi, BSA, PH olc, CIB
Pfc Shigeaki Hirakawa, CIB, GB
Pfc Wallace T. Hironaka, CIB
Pfc Lizo Honma, BS, PH, CIB, GB
Pfc George S. Iha
Pfc Yukio Ige, BSA, CIB, GB
Pfc Henry Y. Ikemoto
Pfc Richard K. Imada, BSA, DUB, CIB, GB
Pfc Wesley H. Ishikawa

My father's signature in the Antitank Company section

p.m. and that he was stunned there were two of us on the same day. It was rare to get descendants of the 442nd as visitors to the cemetery except for special anniversary observations, and it was almost unbelievable there were two of us that day.

Monsieur Freminet arrived with Madame Claudel, the secretary of the organization that is responsible for the Peace and Freedom Trail (Chemin de la Paix et de la Liberté). They too were amazed at my unexpected meeting of Monsieur Canonica and that he had gotten my father's signature in his book as a memento of the 50th reunion. After taking photographs of Monsieur Canonica holding his book, of the page with my father's signature, and of the Bruyères people I had just met, we said our good-byes to the adjutant mayor and Monsieur Canonica. I wished I could have expressed better how deeply grateful I felt for my encounter with them, but I just said softly, "Merci. Merci beaucoup." Then we were on our way to see

Monsieur Canonica and his copy of Orville C. Shirey's
Americans: The Story of the 442d Combat Team

the memorials to the 442nd and the forest where the 442nd
had fought for days to rescue the Lost Battalion. Monsieur
Freminet shared some historical background and information
about each site. We heard stories about the liberation and about
the battle of Bruyères. We saw the 100th/442nd memorial in
the Helladraye forest; we saw the area in Biffontaine where
the Lost Battalion was rescued. We heard stories about how

the young men of Bruyères resisted being forced to join the Germans (stories of escape, going into hiding, joining the French Resistance, and in at least one case, even taking pharmacy concoctions to make one too sick to serve the Germans), how all the villages after Bruyères were burned by the retreating German army, how people remembered the sky was lit by the glow of those fires, and how the people of the Vosges would never forget the valor of the Japanese-American soldiers from so far away. I imagined my father at the places we stopped, both as a young man and fifty years later. We had lunch and thanked Monsieur Freminet and Madame Claudel for showing us the important memorials and battlegrounds. They had been so generous with their time and had been such wonderful hosts on such short notice. Jean-Pierre, Chantal, my friend, and I went on to Épinal American Cemetery. At Épinal, we met Cemetery Superintendent Tom Cavaness, Hideki Obayashi (the husband of the other 442nd descendant from California and a member of Japanese American Living Legacy), and two young French men, Gérôme Villain and Hervé Claudon, who were dedicated to preserving the legacy of the 442nd in the Vosges. The two young Frenchmen talked about growing up listening to their elders talk about World War II and being inspired to pursue learning as much as they could about the 442nd. Hideki was intensely interested in the history of the Nisei soldiers as part of the Japanese-American experience. After Hideki, Gérôme, and Hervé left, we walked through the cemetery, so peaceful with its rows of white crosses and sycamore trees. The afternoon light softened everything, and my friend and I found ourselves assisting in the flag lowering at the end of the day, a ritual neither of us ever expected to be a part of. All was quiet and the air was cool.

After I returned to Hawai'i, I borrowed a library copy
of Monsieur Canonica's book, *Americans: The Story of the
442d Combat Team* by Orville C. Shirey and found out what
the acronyms after my father's name stood for. BSA stands for
Bronze Service Arrowhead; CIB is the Combat Infantry Badge;
and GB is the Glider Badge, which was awarded to those who
trained and fought as glider infantry in the D-Day Invasion
of Southern France. In the book, I also found the listing for
my father's second oldest brother—"Tec/5 Minoru Harada,
CIB." I never knew my uncle had earned a Combat Infantry
Badge. My father never told me about his own military awards
or what he did to earn them. Looking at the book and at the
photos that my parents took on their 1994 tour retracing the
journey of the 442nd, I wonder how my father and the other
veterans felt about returning. They had witnessed the horrors
of war first hand and suffered terrible losses from among their
ranks. Maybe it was good to remember going for broke even
though many memories were painful. Maybe it was good to
see the landscape healed and so different from what they had
seen when they were young soldiers. I can only imagine what
happened to my father the first time he went to Bruyères. The
last time he was there, he left his signature for me to find.

part three

Waiting for Henry

I LIKE THE FEEL OF A CAT'S HEAD, the fur close to the bone. I like the feel of a cat's skull, the shape of it. It is soothing to stroke a cat on the broad flat forehead, feeling the sculpted surfaces under the fur. The tips of a cat's ears are cool. My fingers run through the fur of cats.

I have one lover and one cat. I call my cat Henry after O. Henry and Henry James. My lover is named Jonathan Henry. After his grandfather. Sometimes I call him Henry because it is so much simpler than trying to say Jonathan. And sometimes I call him Jon.

Henry my cat rejects me all the time. Come to me, baby, come to me, lover, I say. He walks away, tail twitching high. I can see his lightly furred two-toned cat balls when he walks away. I think they are so precious. Cat balls are so cute. Henry knows I love him. That is why he can scratch me and make me bleed. That is why he rejects me so much. Cats are like that sometimes.

Jon my lover, the other Henry, is very patient all the time. Sometimes I wonder what he is thinking; he is always so terribly tactful. He is strong but not heavily muscled. Some would call him a "prize catch" (he is a promising medical student), but I would prefer not to look at him that way. Maybe I love Jonathan Henry. He never rejects me. Some people are like that.

During the afternoon, after work, I play with Henry my cat. I rub him and stroke his head. His beautiful head. I tickle his stomach and admire his cute cat balls. I carry him around the house checking the windows. I secure the latches of the screens in the kitchen and the bathroom. I do not want Henry to leave me. I do not want him to be hit by a car.

At night, Henry my lover comes. In the dark, we play out our passions. We become sticky with sweat and fall asleep with the covers off our bodies. Sometimes I feel that Henry my cat is watching us, and I feel embarrassed and somehow wanton. When I make love with Henry the man, I have to close my eyes to enjoy it. I am afraid that if I open them, I will see Henry my cat staring at us, his eyes glowing in the dark.

It is a morning like other mornings. As usual, Henry my lover is ignoring Henry my cat. Henry my lover sits on the couch reading the morning paper. Henry my cat is sitting in the other corner staring at Henry my lover. They are so ridiculous looking, that pair of Henrys. Especially Henry my cat. He looks positively furious, twitching his tail at Henry my lover like that.

Softly I say, teasing, "Henry."

Henry my lover looks at me and says, "Why do you talk to your dumb cat like that? It's abnormal and unhealthy. Stupid cat."

He is not usually so touchy.

Henry my lover has never stroked Henry my cat's beautiful sleek head. He does not like cats. They make him uncomfortable. Perhaps he sees Henry my cat staring with amber eyes at us when we make love at night.

Henry my lover is asking me a very important question, one he has asked me several times before, one which I have never yet answered.

"Crystal, will you marry me?"

"Maybe."

"When?"

"I don't know." I always answer like this. It makes it sound like I do not care. But I do.

"When will you know?"

Jonathan is getting angry. I can tell. He is trying to control his anger. Why doesn't he just swear at me or something? I do not know what to tell him. How should I know when I will be sure? I do not even know if I really love him. What does it mean, to love?

"I don't know when I will know."

A pause. Jonathan looks at me with a suffering face.

"Do you love me?" he asks.

"Yes," I lie. I cannot stand that hurt look in his eyes. I wish he would talk about something else.

"What more is there?"

"It's not that simple," I say.

"Why?"

I pause, feeling the panic in my stomach spread. Sometimes Jonathan makes me feel cornered. He is always demanding that I explain myself to him.

"I don't know you," I say. I feel miserable. I wonder what put these particular words into my mouth. I wish that Henry my cat was here so that I would have something to do with my hands and something to look at besides Henry my lover's face and my feet. I say things that I know will provoke Jonathan. I say things that will hurt him. Is it because these things are true? I say again, "I don't really know you."

He laughs a short bitter laugh. It is a hard, unpleasant sound. Softly he says, "You don't know me." He is incredulous. I am sorry I said that. Now it is his turn to hurt me.

"You say you love me when you don't even know me? You sleep with me without knowing me. Come now, surely you can marry me too without knowing me."

I cannot stand his sarcastic tone of voice.

"No!" I say. "No. You don't understand."

"I don't think I'll ever understand you, Crystal."

I start to cry. I want to scream at Jonathan. How does he know that he loves me? But I am afraid he will say that he really does not love me.

Jonathan holds me gently in his arms.

"I think I love you, Crystal. But if you don't love me, I'm just wasting my time . . . ." his voice trails off. He sounds so sad and tired.

I wish things were nice and perfect. I wish I could say yes and make things simple. Sometimes I wish Jonathan would leave me alone. Sometimes I wish I never got to know him this way.

Henry my lover has left me. I do not like to think about the reasons why he left. I suppose I have driven him to it. Ever since he first started coming at night, in the dark, I have been slowly pushing him away. I was not really aware of what I was doing. Maybe I was just fooling myself into thinking that despite all the trying things about me, Jonathan would still wait for me to make up my mind. Now he is gone.

There was no big quarrel at the end. He was so damn tactful and nice about saying that things had gotten to the point where he did not enjoy being with me. I never meant to annoy him. He told me he thought we should get to know other people who might be more suited to us. He said it would be better for me. I did not cry until he walked out the door. His last words were so trite I would laugh if it did not hurt so much. "We can still be friends," he said before he left. Standard farewell lines. "I'll be seeing you," he said, as if nothing at all had ever happened. I never want to see him again.

Do I love him?

I talk with Henry my cat. I caress his head and tell him silly things. "Oh Henry Henry Henry. You'll never leave me, will you?" He miaows at me. I miaow back at him and laugh.

I spend the night watching television with Henry on my lap. Nothing I watch makes much of an impression on me. I talk to Henry my cat while the television goes on. I predict the eventual outcomes of each situation comedy and each serial. I laugh at the commercials. I tell Henry my cat what a lady-killer he is. I tell him what a handsome handsome tiger he is. I get tired of the television. I take Henry my cat with me to my bedroom. I want to lie down. I find one of Jonathan's socks on the floor by my bed. I start crying. I miss his dark shape and his breathing by my pillow. Henry my cat just looks at me. He purrs and rubs his head against my hand. What would I do without him?

Instead of going to sleep, I play some more with Henry my cat. I cannot sleep. I run through the silent rooms, breaking the stillness with my running feet while Henry my cat chases me. Laughing, I run over the chairs and tables in the living room and the dining room. I leap on the kitchen counters. I laugh as I cavort all over the house with Henry my cat at my heels. It is three o'clock in the morning as the sound of my laughter fades. The house becomes very quiet. I pick up Henry my cat and cradle him like a baby. I think I miss Henry my lover. Suddenly I feel very lonely.

I think I hear noises in the parlor. I go cautiously with Henry my cat to check. It is only the curtain billowing with the breeze and scraping against the lampshade.

Three days later, I come home to an empty house after shopping. Henry my cat is gone. I do not know how he could have left. I am always very careful to secure all the windows before I go out. I open all the cupboards and all the closets. I call for Henry. I run around the house calling for Henry. I wail for Henry Henry. I run around the block calling for him. I walk back to my place, telling myself that Henry is all right and he will come back.

That night I wait for Henry my cat. I try not to think about cars and catnappers. I try not to think of how empty the house is. I do not want my Henry to be squashed to death beneath the wheels of some car. I do not want him to be dissected in some biology class. I do not want him to end up as part of some woman's fur coat. I have kept him so carefully. And now he is gone. He has left me and I am alone.

I hear cats crying nearby. Henry? I run outside and start calling again for Henry my cat. I see the cats but Henry my cat is not with them. I go back inside the house, listening for Henry. There is a faint rustling noise outside. Henry? "Henry!" But it is only the wind blowing the leaves in the trees.

Who would think the night could be filled with such sounds? I hear all the leaves that move with each passing night breeze. I can hear the crickets that are rubbing their wings together and vibrating their dry little bodies.

I fall asleep waiting for Henry. I have a dream. I dream of a black panther who comes near my bed, who comes with the night. His fur ripples over his big panther bones. He glistens in the dark. I am afraid of him. I touch his head. It is smooth. I lose my fear of him in his beautiful head. His fur is thick and seems to perpetually flow over his skull. His eyes are brown, like the eyes of Henry my lover. But this is not Henry my lover. This is a strong panther. He stands by my bed as I stroke his perfect head. His ears are rounded at their cool tips. The fur on his body is also cool. It makes me think of mountain springs and of dew on grass. He is so still. He stands patiently while I run my fingers over his rich black fur.

Henry my cat walks into the room. He is light and glistening. He is so small next to this panther. He is so tiny the panther could probably kill him by simply stepping on him. The panther and Henry my cat start stalking each other. I do not know whether this is a game or not. I watch them gliding in their circles. I watch their immobile cat faces as they slide their soft paws over the smooth vinyl floor. It seems that they will forever glide and slither in their circles on their padded feet. I remember that their velvet paws hide claws.

The panther raises one paw. He raises it like a club. I think he is going to club Henry my cat senseless; he will beat Henry my cat to death. I see the claws coming out of hiding. They gleam and flash. Cats are very clean. I see now that the panther is going to take the life out of Henry my cat with one clean and neat swipe of his claws. I want to save Henry my cat. I cannot move or scream. I am helpless as the panther's paw begins its descent towards Henry my cat. I cannot even close my eyes.

Suddenly, I see that it is the panther who is the victim after all. Henry my cat is under the panther. His tiny claws are moving upward in an arc. He is going to scratch the belly of the panther. I am afraid I will have to see the panther's guts spill out. I am afraid that the pink guts will fall on Henry my cat and suffocate him. The big panther will fall on Henry my cat and crush him. I do not want Henry my cat to die. I do not want the panther to die. I want to save them. Henry my cat's claws flash like little mirrors as they continue upward. The panther's claws look like curved jewels, gleaming with the light of a hundred suns and stars, as they continue downward. I want everything to stop now. I want everything to start over again and end differently. I want everything to stop. Stop. Stop.

When I wake, I hear myself saying Henry Henry Henry. I reach for Henry my lover but he is not here. I want his arms around me. I want him. Why did I lie to him? I told him that I did not love him. Maybe I did not lie to him after all. Maybe I really do not love him. I do not know. Henry Henry. Maybe I mean Henry my cat. I miss Henry my cat. Where did Henry my cat go? How did he go? Henry my cat, if you come back I will feed you good tuna every day. I will let you play outside more often. Henry. Henry my lover, if you come back I will even marry you. I will love you. I will be a good wife. And I will always call you Jonathan instead of Henry. Please come back.

The next morning, over a solitary cup of coffee, I consider an ad I could put in the classified section of the newspaper. "Lost: one cat and one lover. Call ————." People would only snicker. I would be plagued by obscene phone calls all hours of the day and night. Besides, neither Jonathan nor Henry my cat ever reads the classified ads. I rip the ad into little flakes of paper.

I wait for Henry.

The Pond

THE MOTHER BELIEVES THE POND in the backyard is
drying up. It's true there hasn't been enough rain lately and
the new neighbors let the back of their property grow wild so
the California grass is intruding into the spring that feeds the
pond in her backyard. The daughter knows the mother thinks
that people around the daughter's age just don't take care of
their yards the way the old folks used to. But the mother has
done nothing about the pond since her husband died four years
ago, though she wouldn't ever admit it. Sure, she's fed the
few remaining koi every day and made her son install a small
fountain pump to aerate water in the lower pond. But she hasn't
added any new fish to replace the old ones which have died or
been washed away by the few heavy rains since her husband's
death. And she derives no enjoyment from the tranquil beauty
of either the pond or the yard where her husband merged his
artistic sense and his engineering know-how. It has become a
burden to her. When she looks at the pond, the water looks
black to her, not clear at all. She doesn't see the glimmering
orange and gold koi cruising the bottom of the pond or rising up
to skim the surface of the water with their back fins as they have
always done. She rails at her daughter, "Can't you see how dirty
the water is because it's drying up? Can't you see how black it
is? What's going to happen if it doesn't rain soon?" Even when it
rains, she says, "It's not enough." Even when it storms, she says,
"It's not enough." She's worried that the pond is drying up, that
all the fish will die, that her house will fall into ruin.

When the second psychiatrist asks her how her depression
started, she responds slowly, "It - all - started - with - the -
pond." Her voice started to change as she sank deeper and

deeper into the dark sludge of her depression. It turned reedy and thin, tentative and somehow robotic. Her daughter could barely hear her on the phone. The mother lost fifteen pounds in two months, couldn't sleep, grew more and more disoriented. She was convinced she couldn't walk and would totter around the house keeping one leg completely stiff, swaying her body back and forth, right and left, whimpering that she was losing her mind, that she couldn't function, that she was different from everyone else in the world, that she had two pipes in her throat and that pills went down the wrong one, that all the food she ate was no good for her, that everything, everything was terrible. Her behavior got worse whenever her daughter went to pick her up for a doctor's appointment. Her depression actually started before her obsession with the pond, but the psychiatrist doesn't pursue that. It started with her husband's death, but the psychiatrist never gets her to talk about that. He doesn't know about all the things she did well before—how perfect her custard pie was, how fine her needlework and sewing were, how efficient a secretary she had been, what a good wife and mother she was—all he sees is a stubborn elderly Japanese woman who refuses to talk to him.

The second psychiatrist tries Serzone and then Wellbutrin; when neither works he tells the daughter she should seriously consider ECT, electroconvulsive therapy, for her depressed mother. He doesn't know the mother refuses to talk to him because he is middle-aged and blonde and frightening to her. So the daughter takes her mother to another psychiatrist who is middle-aged and Japanese and relentlessly pleasant. The mother hates him, sticks her tongue out at him when his back is turned, and refuses to talk to him about anything. He prescribes Celexa, which also fails to have any discernible effect on her depression. The daughter wants her mother to go to a senior center and do something other than sit in her house doing nothing all day.

The daughter wants her to talk about her grief over losing her husband (the daughter's father), but the mother stubbornly insists that the problem is outside somehow, in the pond, or with the insurance companies which keep changing their names, or with the road she lives on. She piles up her mail and when the daughter goes to the house, the mother pulls out the form letter from her life insurance company and complains, "See, they've changed their name. It's so confusing. How will I remember which company has my policy? I can't function. I can't do ANYTHING." When the daughter drives her mother home from doctor appointments, the mother says with disgust, "Look how dirty the road is. Look how the bushes are all growing onto the road; pretty soon there won't be a road. It's ho-o-orrible." The mother disagrees with everything the daughter says whenever the daughter points out facts or makes observations which run counter to the mother's perceptions of reality. The mother no longer enjoys seeing her friends, who call her frequently and try to visit her, bringing food in their attempts to cheer her up. "They - bring - food - that's - no - good - for - me, I - don't - want - them - to - come," she complains to the daughter in her barely audible voice.

When the son and daughter were children, the pond was filled with koi that swarmed to eat fish food pellets or suck their toes, with crayfish that they caught with dried shrimp and released over and over again, with green bullfrogs that bellowed at night, and brown bufo toads that the daughter would catch and dissect in the interest of science. Water lilies bloomed above the lily pads that floated serenely on the surface. The yard was a little wild, with a large lychee tree and tall mock orange hedges, lots of vegetation to hide behind and crawl into and harvest and smash into mud patties in the children's pretend survival games. Over the years the yard kept changing, gradually becoming less cluttered, more cultivated, more garden-like, with neat rows of periwinkle and pink hydrangea bushes on the terrace above the birds-of-paradise, with flowers and plants that didn't run rampant like the pakalana vines and lantana. The lychee tree was replaced by a small pond and more grass; the mock orange hedges and the dirt trail to the husband's parents' house next door were replaced by more terraces and cement steps. The crayfish and the bullfrogs disappeared mysteriously sometime during the four years the family lived in Japan (the family had to rent the house out and thought the renters ate them). The numbers of koi fluctuated between twenty and forty, then dwindled down to ten after the mother's husband passed away. The mother keeps demanding that her son clear the pond of the water hyacinths. She is afraid their roots will clog the drainage channel and cause the pond to overflow during heavy rain. She complains, "The rappasō is hor-ri--ble. I can't sleep because I have so many worries." She keeps the windows shut tight, refuses to open the sliding shoji doors that would give her a view of the pond and the yard. "Open your windows. There's no light in the house. There's no air," the daughter says. The mother responds, "It's too windy. Do you know how windy it is? Everything will blow around the house." She insists that it's windy when there is no wind, when there has hardly ever been any wind stronger than mild tradewinds where she lives. Even during hurricanes that ripped branches off the trees at the mouth of the valley where she lives, there was minimal damage on her street. The air in her house is still; the walls the color of driftwood isolate her inside her home.

The fourth psychiatrist is a geriatric specialist who talks the recalcitrant mother into attending a program for depressed seniors. The mother tells her sister, "They're shipping me off to Waipahu," so the sister phones her niece (the daughter) to find out what's going on. The mother's sister sees humor in the mother's words and thinks it's witty of the mother to talk of herself as if she's a package getting mailed off to Waipahu. The daughter drives to the mother's house the first morning the program's van is supposed to pick up the mother. There is a message on the mother's answering machine from the driver, who is trying to find her house. The mother had refused to pick up the phone, so the daughter calls the program office and the driver calls her back on his cell phone. Although the mother is not happy about going to the program, she gets in the van and goes to Waipahu. When the daughter calls her that afternoon to see how her first day was, the mother yells, "It's a TERRIBLE place and you're a TERRIBLE daughter for making me go there!" and hangs up. Her voice is normal for the first time in six months. She threatens to never go to Waipahu again, but gets in the van two days later and goes to her program. When the daughter asks the mother what she did at her program that day, the mother says tersely, "Nothing. All they do is eat and drink juice." After she has gone for three days, the daughter asks her again what happens at the program. She replies, "We have classes." The daughter asks what the classes are about, and the mother replies, her voice prickly with irritation, "De-pre-ssion." The next week when the daughter asks the mother about the program, she says, "There's only haoles there." When the daughter insists there must be other people besides haoles, the mother concedes reluctantly, "There are. There are Chinese, Japanese, Hawaiian-Portuguese." She adds, "And lots of haoles and they talk all the time. Talk talk talk. Yak yak yak." When the daughter asks what they talk about, the mother says, "They talk about how angry they are at their daughters." The daughter stops herself from laughing, and replies, "That's good. It's good for people to talk about how they feel sometimes. Are you angry at me?" The mother doesn't answer, and then changes the subject. "What medicine am I taking for my blood pressure?"

The mother still thinks there's something wrong with the pond. She could be right. She doesn't talk about it as much as she used to, but she still thinks it might be contaminated. The daughter finds out from the care coordinator at the program that the mother sits next to another elderly Japanese woman from another valley. The other woman is worried that her mango tree is dead, although her children keep pointing out to her that the tree is alive, like the trees on the mountains, which are green and alive although no one waters them daily with a garden hose. The mother and the other woman worry about the change in the weather, about the dry winter two University of Hawai'i scientists are predicting for the islands. When the two women were younger, in their primes, it rained daily in their valleys—a light rain in the mornings, rain for days on end in the tropical winter. Now it seems the ozone layer is thinner, the sun burns merciless, and only the weeds thrive.

The surface of the pond shimmers in the afternoon sun, shaded by hāpu'u ferns and the mountain apple tree. The koi swim in slow circles and curves in the darkening water, without fear of the impending drought.

The Bakery

THE SUMMER SMELLED OF FRESHLY BAKED CUSTARD
PIES, cinnamon raisin bread pudding, orange zest, sugar, and
vanilla mixed with the smell of tar and hot asphalt. The road
crews were resurfacing Wai'alae Avenue in front of the bakery
Penelope had just started working at, a bakery famous for its
orange cake doughnuts and ice cream cakes. Marlene Ferreira
was the supervisor. She was a very large woman and seemed
to belong in a bakery. Some nurses look like they might exude
ether from their pores if you get too close. Marlene looked like
she might smell of freshly baked bread. She had short wavy dark
hair, green eyes the color of the ocean near the shore, and a little
gap between her front teeth.

Penelope noticed on her first day how many customers
stayed to talk to Marlene. They didn't seem to mind that
the new girl was listening or that other customers were
eavesdropping on their conversations. A man named Rita who
was wearing hot pants and a fuchsia halter top went on for
fifteen minutes about the outrageous cost of silicone breast
implants—"No can believe one breast cost one arm and one
leg. Where I going get dat kine money, honey? Where he stay—
my sugar daddy in shining armor?" Leila the Amway lady
ranted about her divorce and the treachery of her soon-to-be
ex-husband—"All these years I knew something was going on,
but I was too stupid to see it and I jes believed all da lies that
he went throw over me, one net of lies he went throw over me,
one web of deception—I was so trusting, like one lamb to the
slaughter." Lance the skinny local guy who always ordered
seven long johns bragged about his girl troubles—"I get three
girlfriends now. Hard, you know, keeping 'em all happy.

Sometimes I almost say the wrong name cuz they all kinda look alike—short, cute, Japanese." Customers gossiped about their families, friends, and neighbors, confessing all kinds of personal problems as they contemplated the cake doughnuts and cinnamon snails. After a couple weeks, Penelope knew most of the regular customers and their stories better than she knew her parents' neighbors whom she had lived next door to most of her life. She admired the way Marlene made people feel comfortable enough to talk about anything they felt like talking about.

Sharylanne, the other woman who worked Penelope's shift at the bakery, reminded Penelope of a bird. She fluttered and fussed, and her walk was somewhat reminiscent of a hen. She resembled a Kewpie doll and was probably considered "cute" in high school, where she had been a cheerleader. She was thirty-one and constantly worried about her weight, her age, her make-up, and her bleached blonde hair. Sharylanne was married to a man who looked as if he was trying to imitate Elvis Presley. He wore too-tight pants that accentuated his thinness, slicked his hair back with Three Flowers Brilliantine, and let his cigarettes hang petulantly on his lower lip. Penelope had never met anyone like Sharylanne or Sharylanne's husband before.

Business always seemed to slow in the mid-afternoon heat. As Marlene and Penelope watched the traffic through the hazy front window, the road shimmered like a mirage beyond the wedding cake decked with inedible roses in the display case.

"How long has that cake been in the window?" Penelope asked.

"Forevah," Marlene replied. "Mrs. Uehara should put a new one out. She's so picky about keeping the bakery clean, but she doesn't care about making the window look nice. That cake is one antique already."

Penelope nodded. The non-décor of the bakery consisted of a bouquet of faded plastic roses, a vase full of pink feather flowers, a mosaic of a clown from one of those fake broken glass crafts kits, and a dusty old maneki-neko which beckoned wealth to walk in the door with its raised paw.

"There's not much happening out here," Marlene said. "We might as well go back and fold boxes."

The back room of the bakery was large and mostly grey concrete, but the smell of pastries and pies cooling on the racks made it seem warmer and less institutional.

Marlene and Penelope pulled stacks of cardboard from the shelf and started folding boxes. Penelope glanced at the clock.

"Sharylanne is late today. I wonder if something happened."

Just then, Sharylanne came rushing in, flushed and out of breath. "Oh my, I'm so late today. But it wasn't my fault, my husband was late, he didn't tell me he would be late . . . ."

"That's okay, Sharylanne," Marlene said. "Just punch in and don't worry about it."

"I was so worried that you'd be mad at me. I don't know why my husband didn't come home earlier. He knows what time I have to be here. He wouldn't tell me nothing about why he was late." Sharylanne was on the verge of tears. Suddenly, she brightened up. "Guess what! My husband is going to take me dancing tonight. He promised to take me out once a month if I lost some weight. My husband, he's a real good dancer."

Marlene looked up toward the front of the bakery. "Customer, Sharylanne. Can you take care of him?" Sharylanne bounced through the door.

"Honestly. That husband of Sharylanne's," Marlene muttered. "He's always telling her what to do . . . well, maybe she needs somebody like that. Drives me nuts."

Marlene put a stack of finished boxes on the shelf and asked Penelope, "So you going to UH in the fall?"

Penelope shrugged. "Yeah, I guess so."

"You lucky you get to go college. Me, I wish I could go when I was young, but too late now." Marlene smiled. "I been out of school so long, I don't remember how to study."

Penelope shook her head in disagreement. "People go back to school all the time. My aunty is going back to school—to KCC, and she loves it. She studies more than I do."

Marlene just laughed.

Sharylanne had rushed out to serve the customer. He was balding but quite muscular.

"A box of about two dozen pastries," he said. "Just put a couple of everything in there."

Sharylanne started filling the box—two bear claws, two cherry Danish, two cinnamon doughnuts, two of everything. The man suddenly smiled.

"Hey, aren't you Sharylanne Brown . . . uh. . . grad Kaimukī High School?"

Sharylanne looked at him blankly.

"I'm Lee Silva. I don't know if you remember me. I danced with you one dance at da prom," he said. "You wuz so skinny and your hair wuz so long in high school, I almost nevah recognize you."

"Oh yeah, I remember you now," Sharylanne said, although she did not remember him at all. It bothered her that he had indirectly mentioned her weight gain. "You've really changed. What are you doing now?"

"I work for one insurance company," he said.

"I got married," Sharylanne said.

"Me too. Got two kids. How about you?"

"No kids yet." Sharylanne finished filling the box and rang up the total.

"Nice seeing you again."

"You too. See you around."

Sharylanne reached for the phone next to the cash register and dialed. There was no answer at home.

She headed for the back.

Penelope thought Sharylanne had a funny look on her face. Marlene asked, "Is something wrong?"

Sharylanne burst into tears. Penelope and Marlene dropped their boxes. Marlene put her large comforting arm around Sharylanne. Penelope got some Kleenex. She never knew what else to do when an older person started crying. Sharylanne started sputtering, "Th-things aren't so goo-ood at home. I think my husband is seeing a-no-o-ther woman. He called me a fat pig last night." She sobbed uncontrollably.

Penelope thought of telling Sharylanne what scum her husband was, but Marlene spoke first. "Sharylanne, you sure about that? Isn't he taking you out dancing tonight?"

"Y-y-e-es."

"Would he take you out if he was seeing someone else?"

"Maybe not." Sharylanne stopped sobbing. "I don't know why I thought he was cheating on me."

"Why don't you go wash your face and have some coffee? You'll feel better," Marlene said.

As soon as Sharylanne shut the bathroom door, Penelope asked Marlene, "How come you didn't tell her what you think of her husband?"

Marlene shrugged. "I can't tell her that. She's crazy about him. She just has to figure it out herself. I was married once, and I never listened to anybody who badmouthed my husband. Sharylanne won't listen to me. Anyway, even if I don't like Sharylanne's husband, I don't know if he's having an affair, so better I don't say anything."

Penelope nodded. "Yeah, I guess you're right." She wondered how Marlene seemed to know the right things to say and wished she could have that kind of instinct someday.

Marlene and Penelope heard the bathroom door squeak open in the rear of the bakery. "So did you see Rita today in her new red hot pants? She's one man so she has nice small hips and she looks good in hot pants," Marlene said loudly, as if she and Penelope had just been talking about the day's customers all along. "We better go up front again."

Marlene's nephew Kimo sauntered in. "Hey, Aunty," he said, "How're you?"

"Okay. And how's your mom?"

"She's mad at me 'cause I'm against developing Kalama Valley."

"Well, maybe she thinks the farmers can make up their own minds."

"Aunty, if we don't take a stand now, the developers goin' take over everything."

Marlene sighed. She didn't understand what was going on in Kalama Valley. Things just weren't the same anywhere any more. Penelope was busying herself re-arranging the Danish, but was glancing at Kimo thinking he was kind of cute. Marlene noticed how Penelope was discreetly checking out Kimo. Why did these young college kids think being a radical was so cool?

"Anyways, Aunty, Mom wants me to bring home one dobash cake."

Marlene put the cake in its box as Kimo continued talking about Kalama Valley and the struggle for the land. "Kimo, tell your Mom I get this cake."

"No need, Aunty."

"Listen to Aunty." Marlene turned to Penelope. "Can you bring my purse from the back and ring this up? Thanks."

Kimo hesitated. "Okay Aunty. Thanks. Eh, Aunty, you heard 'bout Frankie? He went propose to Edna."

"Well, it's about time."

"Yeah. See you later, Aunty." Kimo smiled and bobbed his chin toward Penelope before he walked out the door.

Afternoon melted into the evening. It was near closing time. The three counter girls consolidated all the remaining pastries onto fewer trays. Marlene mopped. Penelope wiped the display cases. Sharylanne was at the counter when a skinny local Japanese boy in his late teens or early twenties walked in. Although it was a warm night, he was wearing a jacket.

"Can I help you?" asked Sharylanne.

The boy looked nervous. "I'm still deciding."

Penelope looked up at him. He looked vaguely familiar, like a boy she had known in elementary school. He looked at her and then quickly looked away. It was a silly thought, but maybe he was that boy from elementary school and he recognized her too. What was that boy's name? He was fiddling with something in his jacket pocket. Suddenly, Penelope felt apprehensive. Something was not right about the boy. Better not to show any alarm, just keep wiping the glass, she thought. Penelope looked at Marlene, who was still mopping, but who also occasionally glanced up warily at the boy. Only Sharylanne seemed oblivious to the boy's suspicious behavior. She smiled vacantly at the door beyond the boy and drummed her fingers on the display case.

"Gimme two glazed doughnuts," the boy blurted out.

"Is that all?" asked Sharylanne, putting the doughnuts into a bag.

"Uh, no," the boy said, "I still deciding."

Penelope's mind was racing. The boy's eyes seemed wild to her, and unfocused. Was he on drugs? Why was he wearing a jacket when it was so hot? Should she try to nonchalantly go to the back of the bakery and out the service door to get help? Was Marlene having the same thoughts she was having? Marlene was mopping very slowly and deliberately.

"I like two bread pudding too," the boy said.

"Is that all?" Sharylanne asked again.

"Uh, no, gimme two of those too," the boy replied, pointing at the bear claws. "That's it."

Sharylanne put the pastries in the bag and opened the cash register. Penelope saw the boy's hand going for his jacket pocket, and she suddenly said in a voice that seemed to her unnaturally loud, "Didn't you go to Hokulani Elementary?"

The boy looked startled and replied, "Yeah, I went there."

"Mrs. Takahashi's 5th grade class?"

The boy looked at Penelope, narrowed his eyes, then smiled. "I remember you. You were the girl that came from another school in the middle of the year. Ho, you were so quiet." The boy smiled; he didn't look so scary to Penelope any more. "Jesus," he said, shaking his head, "that was a long time ago—Hokulani Elementary. I never think about elementary for so long. Eh, Mrs. Takahashi was one scary teacha, yeah?"

"Yeah, remember her pointy eyeglasses and how she used to yell and hit the desk with her hand when she thought we weren't paying attention?"

"Yeah, was louder than one judge's gavel," the boy said. "Ka-BAM!"

Penelope suddenly remembered the boy's name. "Is your name Jarred?"

"Ho, you get some memory," the boy said.

"You knew the capitals of all the states and all the countries—nobody else knew what the capitol of Burma or Bulgaria was." Penelope didn't know why the boy's ability to identify the names of the capitals of foreign countries had impressed her in 5th grade or why she suddenly remembered it now.

"Rangoon, Burma. Sofia, Bulgaria," the boy said. "Shit, I nevah know I still remember that stuff." He shook his head.

"Sorry, I don't remember your name."

"Everyone used to call me Penny."

"Well, good seeing you, Penny." Jarred turned to Sharylanne. "How much?" He reached into his right pants pocket for his money.

"Nice seeing you too," Penelope said as Jarred paid for his pastries. As soon as Jarred was out the door, Marlene put the mop down and walked over to the counter.

"You know he was going to try rob us," Marlene said.

Sharylanne's eyes widened. "Not! How you know that?"

"He had something in his jacket pocket." Marlene looked at Penelope. "You made him remember who he was when you recognized him from elementary school. You made him remember where he came from before."

"I don't know what made me ask him if he went to Hokulani Elementary. Yeah, I had a bad feeling about him when he first walked in, but then I recognized him. Funny that I suddenly remembered how he knew all the capitals of all the countries in 5th grade."

"Boy, I wonder what people remember about me from 5th grade," Sharylanne said.

"Now there's a scary thought." Marlene laughed. "I'm not going there. We better finish cleaning up. Closing time soon."

Penelope finished bagging all the leftover pastries while Sharylanne threw away the cream-filled doughnuts and Marlene finished counting the money in the register. Then Marlene turned off the neon sign. The night baker came in the back door. He punched in and put on his apron. As the women were punching out, Marlene said, "Hey, Ernie, where you went elementary school?"

"Pālolo. Why you ask? What you wahines was talking about tonight?"

"Fifth grade. 'Night, Ernie."

"'Night, ladies."

Sharylanne was excited about another night out. She ran
straight to the waiting Chevy without looking back. In the
parking lot, Marlene turned to Penelope and said, "You did
good tonight."

"Thanks," Penelope said. "It was weird."

"Sometimes people need help remembering who they are,
where they're from. You did something nice for your classmate
tonight."

"I don't know. Maybe." Penelope hoped Marlene was
right. The night was warm and it started to rain.

"See you tomorrow!"

"'Bye!"

Marlene and Penelope escaped into the shelter of their
cars. Under the street lamps, the raindrops looked like tiny
falling stars streaking in a dark sky before they splashed onto
the glistening black road and the passing cars. As Penelope
started her car, she thought about what Marlene had said.
Maybe that was Marlene's secret, that she somehow reminded
people of who they were, where they were from. Then
Penelope's thoughts dreamily turned to Kimo as she exited the
parking lot and turned onto Waiʻalae Avenue heading for home.
He was kind of cute.

Afternoon at the Psychic's House

INSTEAD OF DRIVING OFF A CLIFF BY THE BLOWHOLE, Stella decided to see a psychic. She had been driving around the island, thinking that it would be so easy to accelerate her car and crash through the guardrail and sail off into those deep blue waters just beyond the cliff. Two weeks ago, she had telephoned her boyfriend/partner/whatever-he-was at work and the secretary had answered, "He'll be back tomorrow—he's on vacation." That was a shock, especially since he had left that morning with his home lunch and briefcase as if it were a normal work day. Then there had been the unpleasant confrontation, and he had cried—why should he be crying when he was the one who was cheating and she was the one who was betrayed? What was that about? She hadn't even told her best friend Bernice anything yet because it hurt too much. She was not eating, not sleeping, but no one knew anything was wrong. Every morning she put ice on her eyes and then applied her make-up. She smiled a lot at work as if everything was positively hunky-dory, but she felt like she was holding everything together so tightly in a white-knuckle way she was going crazy. She wanted to feel different. That's why now she found herself looking at the footwear on the front porch of what seemed to be a typical middle class post-World-War-II single-wall construction local house surrounded by brown grass and some scraggly pīkake bushes. She caught herself staring a little too long at a pair of polished dark brown men's Ferragamos, a pair of Evan-Picone black leather women's pumps with 2-inch heels, a pair of well-worn Nikes with pink shoelaces and purple trim, a pair of larger Nikes with standard white laces and black trim, a pair of small black grunge boots, a pair of well-worn beige vinyl orthopedic sandals, and a

scattering of rubber slippers which reminded her of jelly beans—
blue, black, pink, in children's and adults' sizes. Stella added her
pewter Aerosoles to the array.

Since that horrible revelation, everything felt surreal. Stella
felt her life was stuck in some kind of twilight zone doldrums—
she hated that feeling of going nowhere, sitting dead in the
water, no wind, no land in sight, no real destination—only miles
and miles of ocean that seemed like an expanse of nothingness
instead of ultramarine beauty. She found it impossible to make
a decision about what to do. Someone at work had mentioned
Linh the psychic whose powers were becoming legendary in
Honolulu. Stella had had no idea how to find the house or what
the woman's last name was. She had heard the house was in
Kaimukī or Kapahulu. She had guessed that the psychic's last
name was a common Vietnamese surname, had looked at all the
phone numbers with the appropriate area prefix, and had chosen
the one she thought was most likely. She had felt foolish when
she had asked the person who answered the phone, "Hello. Is
this Linh the psychic's house?" It was, but she would have to
wait two months for an appointment. Her other option was
just to drop in and wait until the appointments were finished.
"Cannot guarantee Linh will see you. You just gotta wait. Better
come early. Some people come 6:00 in the morning wait in line,"
the voice at the other end had said.

So there Stella was, on the threshold, with no appointment,
staring at footwear. She could still leave and go somewhere
else. She had disregarded the instructions about coming early.
It was 2:00 in the afternoon. She decided to leave it to fate—if
she was meant to see the psychic, she would. If there were too
many other people and the psychic did not have time to see her,
well, maybe that meant she'd just have to figure things out on
her own. She was a rational person, who grew up believing in
science, in evidence, in the primacy of logic. So what was she

doing here? It wasn't as if she was going to believe whatever the psychic said. It wasn't as if she was going to let a psychic dictate what she did with her life. What was she doing here?

Stella crossed the threshold. The rooms in the front of the house had that just-cleaned, stripped look as if the occupants had just moved out. There were no books on the bookshelves. There was a long dining room table but no chairs. There were no curtains on the windows. Down the hallway, Stella saw a glass door and what looked like another entrance. When she reached the glass door, she could see that the connection between the old front of the house and the remodeled back of the house was actually the waiting room, a transitional space between the old house and the new extension. Three Vietnamese kids were sprawled in front of the television watching *The Flintstones*. There was a closed wooden door at one end of the waiting room. A notepad was set slightly askew on a black lacquer coffee table near the door. "SIGN IN HERE" was printed at the top of the notepad, and there were two columns labeled "Appointment" and "Walk In." The column of walk-ins was nearly full. Stella wrote her name on the pad and sat down between the middle-aged man she assumed was the owner of the Ferragamos and the skinny teenager with black lipstick who was most likely the owner of the petite grunge boots. A pretty local hapa girl and a tan, athletic-looking haole boy (the Nike couple) sat close to each other. A pleasant-looking local woman in her late twenties or early thirties and an older Hawaiian woman in a green muʻumuʻu sat across from Stella. They looked like relatives. Stella decided the older woman in the green muʻumuʻu owned the beige orthopedic sandals and that the younger woman probably owned one of the pairs of rubber slippers. The wearer of the corporate pumps was probably the one in consultation with the psychic behind the closed wooden door. Stella noticed the black velvet painting of Mary, the Virgin

Mother, which seemed incongruous next to the television. The clock in the shape of Vietnam on the opposite wall was ten minutes ahead of Stella's watch.

"You get one appointment?" the older woman in the green muʻumuʻu asked Stella.

"No." Stella shook her head.

"Oh good." The woman smiled. "The man, he get one appointment, and everybody else just waiting. We been waiting almost three hours already because had plenny people with appointments before us. We're next, after the man, if nobody else comes with appointments."

"Oh." Stella attempted a weak smile and nodded. "I heard that you have to wait a long time sometimes."

Everyone watched the television absent-mindedly because it was on. The children didn't look as if they belonged to anyone in the room. Maybe they were the psychic's relatives. They were very quiet and well behaved. Stella wondered what life would be like having a psychic for a grandmother or aunt. Maybe the children didn't think about it because they had never known any other life. Could they have secrets the psychic did not know about? Did the psychic always know what they were thinking and doing? Did she predict their future careers and relationships for them? Did she warn them of impending personal disasters?

The credits for *The Flintstones* rolled by. The children went outside. The Nike couple gazed into each other's eyes the way young lovers sometimes do. The Ferragamo businessman got up, paced a 4-foot length of floor, leaned against the wall, sat down briefly, and got up again. The older woman in the muʻumuʻu asked Stella, "Is this your first time to come here?"

Stella nodded. "Yes. How about you?"

"First time. My daughter's friend came here and she said Linh the psychic lady said plenny things that came true. Pua, tell about your friend."

Pua leaned forward a little. "It's true. My friend wanted a baby and she and her husband had been trying so hard, but no baby. So my friend came to see what Linh would say. And Linh told her all kinds of stuff about her job and her family. And then, Linh looked at her and asked her if she had a boyfriend. My friend was shocked because she's married. And Linh asked her, 'You sure you don't have boyfriend? You don't fool around?' And my friend said she would never cheat on her husband. How come Linh was asking her a question like that? And Linh told her, 'Because you going to have a baby, but the father not your husband.' So my friend didn't believe anything Linh told her because the idea that she would cheat on her husband was so outrageous to her."

"So did she have an affair?" Stella asked.

"Her? No way." Pua paused. "Two years later, after they tried in vitro and all kinds of other stuff, my friend went to a sperm bank. She got pregnant and had a baby. And Linh was right. Her husband is not the baby's biological father."

"I heard she tells people what kind of car they're going to own," the girl with the black lipstick said. "She told my friend she was going to own a Mercedes Benz. Unreal. That would be so cool to own a Mercedes."

"I heard she warns people about car accidents," Pua's mom said.

"My friend told me this really spooky story," the Nike couple girl said. "Her sister's friend's cousin heard the story from her friend. This lady wanted to see Linh, but she was afraid and wanted her friend to go with her. So her friend came with her to see Linh, but she didn't want a reading. So Linh told the lady who wanted the reading all kinds of things, and I guess the friend got curious as she was listening. So at the end of the first lady's reading, the friend asked about her own future. And Linh just looked at her and said, 'I don't see a future for you' or

'You have no future' or something like that. She wouldn't take the friend's money. And then, the next day, the friend was in a car accident and died."

Stella felt a slight chill. The Nike couple boy looked sort of uncomfortable and shifted in his seat. "It's just a story," he said. "It was just a coincidence. Do you always have to tell that story?"

Pua's mom shook her head. "I don't know if it was such a good idea to come here."

The businessman said, "I just come for business advice."

Pua's mom looked at the businessman. "So you came here before? What does she do in there?"

"She does different things. Sometimes she makes you pick cards. Sometimes she just talks."

"Is it okay to ask questions?" Pua asked.

"I let her talk first. Then I ask questions," the businessman replied.

"She must give you good advice if you come back," Pua's mom said.

"Yes, sometimes she tells me things I didn't think about before. Sometimes she confirms my hunches," the businessman said.

A woman in a purple silk dress came into the waiting room. She was very pretty and very flashy. Stella thought there was something about her make-up and diamond jewelry that made her look like a Korean bar hostess.

"You have an appointment?" Pua's mom asked the woman in the silk dress.

"Yes, I have 3:00 appointment," the woman said with a slight accent.

"Oh well, guess we got to wait a little longer," Pua's mom sighed. The wooden door opened and a tall, middle-aged blonde woman in a bright red suit walked out briskly. She looked upset, on the verge of tears. A petite young Vietnamese woman came out and asked, "Who's next?" Stella was surprised at how young the psychic was. She had expected an elderly, wizened grandmother. She had expected grey hair pulled back in a bun and a face ravaged by time and war. The psychic was almost glamorous—she looked as if she could be a Vietnamese actress, like the ones Stella saw on the movie posters in Chinatown, in the windows of the stores and restaurants along River Street. She looked like a Chinese beauty queen, like the ones Stella remembered seeing on cracked seed boxes when she was a kid. Stella was struck by her eyes, which were large and beautiful, but somewhat mournful. Was she a boat person? Stella wondered. The businessman went into the office and closed the door.

Pua's mom said, "That lady is the third person I seen today that came out of that room looking unhappy. Only one lady looked happy today. Everybody else that came out, you couldn't tell what they were thinking. Their faces didn't have any expression. Couldn't tell anything from their faces."

That was to be expected, Stella thought. It was like a doctor's office waiting room—the exiting patients didn't look directly at the patients who were still waiting to see the doctor and kept their expressions carefully neutral. Also, Stella thought, probably most of the people who came to see Linh were upset to begin with. They were in some kind of crisis, like she felt she was, and they didn't want to make another mistake. Or maybe they wanted to hear something hopeful—that they actually had something good to look forward to. Someday, something good. Maybe Linh told them things that confirmed what they already thought, so they were upset because they had wanted her denial of what they thought instead of confirmation. It occurred to her that except for the Ferragamo businessman, she couldn't tell why the people waiting with her at that moment were there to see Linh. What did they want to hear? What did she want to hear?

The girl with the black lipstick said, "I heard that she gets tired in the afternoon. One of my friends who came early in the morning told me everything Linh said was true. Another friend who came in the afternoon said she was way off. Just totally wrong."

"I heard the same thing from this lady I work with," Pua's mom said.

The Nike girl and boy were whispering to each other. The young man kept looking at his watch and then at his girlfriend. Finally they got up. The girl smiled a half-smile at the remaining people in the waiting room as she and her boyfriend left. The boyfriend didn't acknowledge anyone. Stella thought, well, they apparently didn't have a crisis they needed to resolve immediately.

Pua's mom said, "I heard the psychic lady donates all the money people give her to her church."

Stella wondered if Linh was a Catholic because of the picture of the Virgin Mary on the wall. Maybe it wasn't so strange. After all, weren't Catholics the ones who were into mystery? Stella tried to remember what she had read about Catholicism. There were no Catholics in her family, so she had to rely on things she had read.

Pua's mom asked the woman in the purple silk dress, "You been here before?"

The woman nodded. "Yes. Many times. Since seven years ago, I come once a year."

Pua leaned forward. "So, things she told you came true?"

The woman smiled. "I don't know if all came true. But some things she tell me, I believe."

"If all the things Linh said haven't come true, why do you keep coming?" Stella asked.

The woman looked thoughtful. "Seven years ago, I came with my friend. She was pregnant and wanted to know if her baby would be okay. Linh told her something wrong with her baby. Something wrong with her baby's heart. Linh said her baby would die before two years old. My friend was so upset. I told my friend, maybe Linh was not right, maybe she make mistake. But my friend wouldn't listen me. She cry cry cry all the time. Made her husband crazy. Made everyone crazy. I thought it was bad idea to see Linh, but was too late. I told my friend see the doctor. The doctor said nothing was wrong, everything okay, don't worry so much. Bad for the baby worry so much. My friend still believe Linh.

"After couple weeks, my friend decided that she would find out everything about babies with bad hearts. She was . . . what's the word? . . . obsessive. She try to read everything about heart conditions in babies. I was worry about her, but this was better than she only cry. Only thing, she only want to talk about what she read. If I telephone her, she only talk about heart problems. I still think Linh make mistake, but my friend still didn't listen me.

"Then, my friend she decided she must find best heart surgeon for her baby, so she research all the doctors. She ask everybody who best doctor was in Hawai'i. She even ask about mainland specialists. She only talk about doctors. If she meet a doctor, she ask who was good heart specialist. She make list, look newspaper articles, ask her attorney friends which doctors been sued malpractice. I never thought about such things.

"All the time, she getting bigger and bigger. No problem with pregnancy. Pretty soon, she gave birth to baby girl. Nothing wrong with her baby. Beautiful baby. I thought, Linh make mistake, but I didn't tell my friend that. Then, after about one month, her baby got sick. Very serious. The sickness damaged her baby's heart. But my friend was ready. She knew which doctor to go. She knew everything about heart problem."

Pua leaned forward. "So, the baby lived?"

The woman in the purple silk dress nodded. "Oh yes. She's so cute. But maybe she would have died if my friend didn't do everything she did."

Pua's mom said softly, "So, your friend changed her baby's destiny."

"Wow," the girl with the black lipstick said. "Like I never thought about that. I thought you just go to Linh and she tells you what's going to happen and if it's true, it just happens. And when it happens, you think, oh yeah, Linh said it was going to happen and I guess I got a good reading because what she said was true. Or you see Linh because you're trying to decide about something like should you break up with your boyfriend and she tells you the best thing to do. And you do it, and things work out, so you figure she was right." She flushed and smiled sheepishly, as if she had just revealed her secret. Oh my God, Stella thought, I'm a dingbat like this Goth girl.

"Does your friend see Linh every year too?" Stella asked the woman in the silk dress.

"No. My friend very superstitious. She think it's not good to come for just curiosity. She think she only come when she has big question. Since she came to ask about her baby seven years ago, she never came back yet. She think no need come back yet."

"Do you come with a big question every year?" Stella asked.

"Everybody different. I'm not like my friend."

The door opened, and the businessman walked out in a very business-like way. His expression was neutral. Stella couldn't tell how he felt. But then, he was there just for business advice. Linh came out from her office, looked at directly at Stella, and asked, "Who's next?"

"I am," the woman in the purple silk dress said. She got up and followed Linh into her office.

Pua's mom said to Stella, "The psychic lady looked at you. She thought you were next."

"You think so?" Stella said, feeling somehow like denying the look Linh had given her. Was it a good sign or a bad one? If Linh really was psychic, she should know who was next. Or was it possible that Linh sensed something about Stella that caught her attention? Stella wondered whether she should continue waiting or leave, and found curiosity more compelling than fear. But what if the psychic told her something that she couldn't deal with? What if there was no hope of things working out well? The afternoon sun seemed to illuminate the psychic's closed door. Stella decided to wait for her turn to see what was on the other side.

About an hour later, the woman in the purple silk dress emerged. Her face was calm and impenetrable. "Next," the psychic called, looking directly at Stella again. Pua and her mother got up and followed the psychic into her office.

Stella was left with the girl with the black lipstick. When Pua and her mother emerged from the psychic's office, they looked satisfied. The girl with the black lipstick went in and stayed in for only fifteen minutes. She avoided looking at Stella as she exited the waiting room. "Next," the psychic called. Stella got up and followed Linh into her office.

The office was almost Zen-like in its minimal décor, which consisted of a small round table and some chairs. There was a deck of playing cards on the table. The way Linh looked at her made Stella feel a little uncomfortable. Linh's dark brown eyes seemed so large and serious. Linh pointed at the cards and said, "You shuffle." Stella shuffled the cards, which felt stiff and new. "Cut the cards—three times—here, here, here," Linh said, pointing at three places on the table. Stella did as she was told. Linh started flipping over cards—seven of spades, queen of diamonds, jack of clubs, deuce of hearts—the cards were revealed quickly and just as quickly were covered by the next card.

"You live in house—two buildings on property—garage one building? Get a tree on side of house. You get one brother, one sister. You drive small car? You very strong, very strong." Linh spoke very fast with a heavy accent, so Stella had to concentrate to understand. Linh was wrong—she didn't have a sister; there was no tree on the side of her house. What did Linh mean about her being strong? Linh went on. "You very sad very sad. No kill yourself." Stella was taken aback. Linh paused and looked at her again in that disconcerting way. "You are good person," Linh said. "Your boyfriend, he love you. He not love another woman. He love you. He come back to you—three weeks." Linh paused, briefly staring into space, and continued, "Three months—three years—thirtee . . . " Linh's voice trailed off, "years. He come back."

Stella was stunned. What was the psychic trying to tell her? To wait? Thirteen years or thirty years? Linh went on, "You be nice to him, he come back." What did she mean—was she supposed to stand by her man? Linh looked at her again. "He cannot find anyone as good as you. He come back." Stella felt an empty dull ache in the pit of her stomach. She suddenly realized that what she really wanted to hear was that she would meet someone else and live happily ever after, but the psychic wasn't telling her that. "He come back. You going be very successful your job. You very smart." Linh was switching topics, talking fast, something about many papers, something about a Ph.D. "You going to move three more times in your life. Three big moves in your life. Go another country. You job very good. You very strong. Someone your ancestor watching you. Maybe father maybe grandfather. You going to own two houses. One house you sell. You have question?"

Stella swallowed and said softly, "So you think I should stay with my boyfriend?"

"He love you very much," Linh said.

Stella felt Linh's eyes staring at her and was almost afraid to say, "Can't I meet someone else?"

"Your boyfriend love you. You very strong. God take care you. You have question?"

Stella didn't know what to say, so she just shook her head. She did not think God would take care of her. She didn't go to church and didn't believe in formal religion. The reading was over. She had heard that most people gave Linh sixty to eighty dollars, so she put her money on the table. To her surprise, Linh said, "Too much. You keep. God take care you," took one twenty dollar bill, and pushed the other bills back towards Stella. Was this a good sign or a sign that her situation was worse than she thought? Stella thanked Linh and walked out of the office. A young woman in a green tank dress and a middle-aged woman who looked like a schoolteacher were in the waiting room. Stella had no idea what her face looked like to the two women who were waiting, but she found herself thinking of the story the woman in the purple silk dress had told about her friend who had changed her baby's fate. It was only five o'clock in the afternoon, but Stella suddenly felt hungry. She noticed the faint fragrance of pīkake as she left the yard and headed toward her car trying to make sense of what Linh had said, but the words felt like clouds shifting shapes and dissipating into the troposphere, leaving only sky.

Into the New Millennium

ELISE WANTED TO BELIEVE IN REINCARNATION, maybe because her father had told her when she was six years old that he doubted the existence of God, heaven, and hell. He didn't believe in reincarnation either and had told her that people just turn to nothing after they die—no afterlife, no heaven or hell, no reincarnation—people just turn to dust. She wondered what being dust would feel like, but it was too scary to imagine nothingness as she lay awake in the dark, watching shadows flickering on her bedroom wall.

She suspected there was no reincarnation after divorce either. Her friends picked themselves up after their breakups and moved on with their lives. What was wrong with her? Her friend Sarah advised her, "It's okay to be angry at him. It's okay to curse him," but it made her feel worse every time she screamed at his absent person in the car. Even his mother had told her, "There's something wrong with him. You're lucky you're still young and you have a job. You can go on with your life. You can meet someone else. Not like me—I had to stay married to raise the children, and I didn't have a job. So I stayed married." Elise felt sad when she heard that, but then she thought maybe it had been the best choice for her ex-mother-in-law, who actually appeared to be content with her life.

So now Elise's friends were busy throwing men into her path whenever they could.

"My mother wants you to go out with my brother," her friend Brenda announced at lunch at Hee Hing two weeks after the divorce was finalized.

"He's engaged," Elise responded, stabbing a succulent har gau with her chopsticks. "Besides, he's not my type."

"My mother wants you to seduce him so that he breaks his engagement with that haole fiancée of his," Brenda persisted as she dissected her bean curd roll, pulling out the plump black mushroom pieces and popping them into her mouth.

"Jesus, Brenda, tell your mom to stop being a racist. It's the new millennium. Anyway, you know I don't go around seducing men. I'm the one who has to get seduced."

"I know. You're both so goddamn passive! He would never make the first move—that's why that haole hooked him. She just hooked him and reeled him in. He nevah even put up one fight. He nevah seen the fishing line hanging out of his mouth—he nevah even feel the hook in his lip." Brenda poked a pork siu mai with her chopsticks and dipped it in her mustard soy sauce. "If my son Brandon ever fall victim like my brother to any woman like that, whether she haole or local, I going to choke him. Elise, can't you try to be more aggressive? Can't you make the first move for a change?" Brenda sighed as she motioned for the waitress with a different dim sum cart toward their table. "Let's get those spinach shrimp things, okay?"

Brenda's cell phone rang and she answered. "Hello? . . . Yeah yeah, I eating at Hee Hing. Okay . . . Okay . . . Bye." She stuck the cell phone back in her bag. "That was Darren. That husband of mine always thinking about food. He like me bring home some dim sum. I tell you, it's so convenient to have one cell. You should get one."

Elise shook her head. "Nah, I don't really need it."

Brenda waved her chopsticks at Elise. "You are the only person I know who no more one cell phone yet. You are the only woman I know who nevah been to Vegas yet. What kine local girl you?"

Sarah and Elise were browsing through the CDs at Borders. "Elise, there's someone I want you to meet. He's my new renter.

He's really nice. He has a good heart—I can tell."

"How old is he?" Elise was well aware of Sarah's penchant for younger men.

"He's older—I know you don't like younger men—but not too old, maybe ten years older than you. Tall, kinda cute . . . blonde with a ponytail."

"Sarah, he sounds like an old hippie from Kaua'i."

"Well, yeah, he did live on Kaua'i for a while, but he's not an old hippie. He's just, well, a little unconventional, but I can tell, he's very kind. Very kind. And he writes poetry. Like you."

Elise groaned. "I don't think so, Sarah. I don't think he's my type. What if I hate his poetry? It will never work. What does he do?"

"He's an attorney. But he's not like other attorneys."

Elise groaned again. "Sarah, I don't think so. He sounds like a refugee from the sixties, he writes poetry, and he's a lawyer. Three strikes—he's out."

"Okay, but think about it. Just think about it."

The phone rang. It was Kimiko, who had moved to Hoboken, New Jersey, from Wahiawā ten years before. "Well, I did it. I told Roger that he had to make a choice—it's either his wife or me. He can't have us both—I can't stand it any more. He always says he's going to leave her, but something always comes up. For three years he's been telling me he's going to leave her as soon as he has enough money. First he's working on some big business deal that's going to make it possible for him to leave, then he's got to sell their vacation cottage on the Cape first. He has no balls. What do I need with a man who has no balls? I would rather be alone than be with a man who makes me feel alone!"

"Well, it's about time," Elise said.

"Yeah, I know, I know. I know you had reservations about

him but you didn't want to say too much. I know I know."

"So what did he say?"

"He looked all miserable and told me he couldn't leave his wife because she has colon cancer. I felt bad, but then I thought, what if he's lying to me?"

"You think he'd lie about something like that?"

"Well, I remember that he told me a story about how he had once cheated on his wife with one of her acquaintances, then had lunch with the woman's husband. When his wife accused him of sleeping with the other woman, he reprimanded her, pointing out to her that he had just had lunch with the husband and had found out the woman had some serious medical condition that he couldn't reveal. He asked his wife how he could possibly have lunch with the woman's husband if he was sleeping with the woman."

"And you still went out with him even after he told you that? Didn't you wonder about him after hearing that story?"

"I was stupid—he was so intelligent and sensitive, and I thought we had such a deep connection somehow—like he knew he could tell me anything and that he could trust me to understand him, that he was really interested in me and that I could talk to him about anything."

Elise understood what Kimiko was talking about. After all, that's how she had felt about her ex-husband. Which was why she couldn't move on. Which was why she didn't think she'd ever find anyone who would make her feel that way again. She didn't think Kimiko would move on yet either. At least, not yet.

"What if he comes back and tries to sleep with you again?" Elise said. "What if he tries to make up with you without leaving his wife?"

"It's over unless he leaves Monique," Kimiko said, but Elise could tell her friend's resolve was already weakening.

It was 5:30 in the morning Hawai'i time when Elise turned

on the television, saw one of the World Trade Center towers burning, black smoke billowing, and saw the second plane hit the second tower on the morning news. She called Brenda.

"Hello?" a sleepy Brenda answered the phone.

"Turn on your TV."

"Why?"

"Just turn in on."

"Okay, I got the remote here." There was a pause. "Oh my God . . . oh my God . . . are we in a war?"

It was two days before Elise could get through to Kimiko. The phone lines were busy. On Thursday, she got through.

"It's horrible here," Kimiko said. "A lot of the people who worked in the World Trade Center lived around here. It's so sad—my friend's cousin had just started working there—he's missing. There's a couple down the street who both worked there and are missing too. One of the neighbors is taking care of their dog. It's so sad."

"Some people from Hawai'i died. There was a pastry chef who worked at Windows of the World who's missing. There were also two women who were passengers on that plane that crashed in Pennsylvania," Elise said. "All I do is watch the coverage on television. There are no airplanes in the sky here— it's weird. It's so quiet."

"I saw the towers burning before they fell," Kimiko said. "I was on my way to work and there were all these cars at the lookout point that gives you a view of Manhattan from Hoboken and all these people were looking toward Manhattan so I stopped to look too. Oh my God, I thought, and then I drove to work to tell everyone there that the Twin Towers were on fire. My friend Susan wanted to see, so we drove back to the lookout, but by the time we got there, the Towers were gone and there was just this huge cloud of smoke. The people at the lookout were in shock. Everyone was wondering what was going on. Now people here are saying the news isn't showing how bad it really is. They're just showing the area where the towers used to be—I heard the destruction covers a much bigger area."

"The news keeps showing the towers burning, then falling, and that huge dust cloud engulfing everyone and everything in its path over and over—and that church graveyard covered with ash and papers—papers with personal information—bits of people's lives blowing through the streets of Lower Manhattan."

"I heard people who were trapped in the towers were leaving messages on their families' voicemail and answering machines," Kimiko said softly. She sounded as if she were about to cry.

"Have you noticed that you don't see Dick Cheney at all or hear anything at all about him?" Elise said. She didn't know why she suddenly thought of something so irrelevant.

"Maybe he's dead."

"They just say he's at an 'undisclosed location,' but I bet he had a heart attack and they're afraid to say anything yet."

On Sunday, Elise called Kimiko. "Dick Cheney's alive," she said. "I heard him on the radio."

"They can't find any survivors. The search dogs are getting depressed," Kimiko said. "My friend Leah is looking for her youngest cousin, who had just started working for Cantor Fitzgerald. The immediate family can't handle the bureaucratic red tape or the long lines, so she's handling it. It's so sad—all those people holding pictures of their missing loved ones, all those photos of the missing tacked up on walls. I feel as if the city is full of grief. It's horrible here."

Kimiko went on. "There's a terrible burning smell, but also another smell—I think it's the smell of death. I can't get away from it. Every day I see that big cloud of smoke that's just hanging there over Ground Zero."

Elise thought no one would ever get away from it. A week after the attack, planes were back in the air space above Honolulu. Elise called Kimiko.

"I saw a plane today. It was creepy. It made me nervous."

"Yeah, it makes me feel funny too. The lights are on all night at Ground Zero because they're trying to recover the bodies. It feels like I'm looking at the spirits of the dead when I look at that cloud of dust glowing above Lower Manhattan like that. That cloud is probably ashes of all those people who died. It's eerie—it just hovers above Ground Zero and won't go away." Even though Ground Zero was so far away, it felt to Elise that nothing would ever be the same.

Just before Christmas, Kimiko called. "I broke up with Roger."

"I'm sorry," Elise said, but she wasn't sorry about the break-up; she was sorry that Kimiko was feeling bad. "But it's the best thing. I'm glad you finally did it."

"I asked him who he'd call on his cell phone if he knew he had only one last call to make, and he said he'd call me of course, but I knew he was l-y-y-in-ng." Kimiko started sobbing loudly into the phone. "I kn-n-ew in my heart that he would call his w-i-i-i-fe."

"Oh Kimiko, you don't want him if he wouldn't make his last call to you." Elise started feeling weepy too, thinking of all those stories of people calling their loved ones one last time, thinking of the dust cloud that lingered above Ground Zero. "You need a man who would definitely make his last call to you."

Kimiko was bawling into the phone now. "Yes yes yes, We

need someone who will want to make his last call to us! We need someone we would make o-o-ur last call to-o-o."

"But w-we d-don't even ha-a-ave cell phones," Elise sobbed back.

"We don't even ha-a-ave cell phones," Kimiko wailed. Then she started wheezing and Elise couldn't tell if Kimiko was laughing or crying. "Do you know how ri-ri-diculous we sound?" Kimiko sputtered. "We don't even ha-a-ave cell phones!" Elise started laughing so hard she couldn't talk.

When Kimiko could talk again, she said to Elise, "If I had a cell phone and I knew I didn't have much time left, I would call you."

"My brother's fiancée goin' move back to Texas," Brenda announced at lunch in August. "She wants to be with her family."

"There. You see? She can't be that bad if she loves her family that much," said Elise.

"Yeah, she not so bad, I guess. I don't know what my brother going do. Maybe now you can make your move."

Elise laughed. "You're terrible, Brenda. Stop it already."

Brenda was examining the menu. "Hmmm. This garlic ahi sounds 'ono. Or maybe the seafood linguine in spicy marinara sauce. You sure you don't want to go fishing for my brother?"

"Brenda, that would be bachi. Not good to go after someone else's catch. What comes around goes around."

"You're so superstitious. Get with the new millennium. I bet you still nevah get one cell phone, even after hearing all those stories about people making their last calls to loved ones on their cells. Every time I think about them, I feel like crying. Even now, almost a year later."

Elise was on her way to work listening to NPR and getting

weepy again. A woman who had lost her husband in one of the Twin Towers was talking about how she felt that September 11th had lasted a whole year, and that finally, one year later, she felt as if September 12th was finally coming. There was talk of a memorial of some kind, but no one seemed to know what that memorial should be. Dawn lit the clouds in the eastern sky a pale topaz and carnelian above Koko Head as Elise headed to work. Even to her, it had seemed like a very long year. How did people manage to go on?

"Sorry, I got stuck in traffic," Brenda said. "If you had one cell phone, I could have called you to tell you I was going to be late. Anyway, happy birthday, you dinosaur. This morning was so nuts I forgot your present at home. Someone going bring 'em here for me."

"That's okay, you can give me my present later."

"Nah, it's coming already."

Elise and Brenda got a table with a view of Ala Moana Park. It was sunny and the sky was blue and cloudless.

"My brother's fiancée went back to Texas and went rekindle the flame with her old high school sweetheart. How dare she dump my brother!" Brenda said indignantly as she spread aioli butter on her focaccia.

"Geez, Brenda, I thought you wanted them to break up."

"Yeah, but I wanted him to dump her, not the other way around." Brenda was waving to someone by the entrance of the restaurant. "Good—your present is here. My brother is my delivery man today and he has accomplished his mission." Brenda ignored the look that Elise gave her. "Tanks, Brian." Brenda took the lavender gift bag from Brian. "You know Elise."

"Hi Elise. Happy Birthday."

"Thank you. I told Brenda I didn't need to have my present

today, but she already called you."

"Open it," Brenda said.

Elise pulled a pink box out of the gift bag. Inside the box was a hundred dollar bill. "God, you're giving me money for my birthday like my parents!"

"Your friend Kimiko went call me at work from New Jersey. Resourceful, that girl. This is from her and me. After lunch, we go cell phone shopping. You know that Nokia has da coolest new phone—first one with a built-in camera. You can take one picture with your phone and send it to someone. Das da one you should get. Sorry you going get one more bill to pay, but you not going be behind the times any more, girl. You gotta move on with the rest of us." Brenda turned to her brother. "E Brian, you might as well stay and eat with us since you're here already."

"If it's okay with Elise. You know, maybe you two want more girl time."

Elise smiled at Brian. "We get too much girl time. Stay. Have lunch with us. We just ordered."

"Yeah, Brian. And after lunch, come help us choose one cell phone for Elise," Brenda said. Elise could not believe Brenda was actually trying to play matchmaker.

Brian pulled out a chair to sit down. "Ho, Brenda. You was never the subtle type. No worry, Elise. I know Brenda as well as you do."

The three of them were laughing and telling stories about how bad Brenda was at concealing her ulterior motives and true feelings when the waitress arrived with another place setting— white porcelain plate, black napkin, fork, spoon, and knife. The restaurant was full of people and noise, the trees in the park full of sunlight and shadows. Beyond the park, Elise could see the ocean. She decided Kimiko had to be the first person she would call with her new cell phone.

Do You See What I See?

DAD WOULD HAVE DISAPPROVED of the funeral service
Mom was having in his memory, Penelope thought, watching
her daughter Keala, who hadn't shed a single tear at her favorite
grandpa's funeral. He would have disapproved of Mom's
decision to have a 21-gun salute at the burial at the urging of
the well-meaning aunties. He had ordered in his no-nonsense
samurai way, "Don't bother people with a long funeral service.
Don't even put an obituary in the newspaper." Maybe he'd
forgive them if he was watching; maybe he'd know the service
was actually for those who were left behind. Maybe he'd be
secretly pleased that they were making such a fuss over him. The
young soldier's gloves were flawlessly white against the perfectly
folded burial flag's blue field of stars. Penelope looked at her
mother. Mrs. Miyamura's head was bowed and tears welled
up in her eyes as the young soldier offered official condolences
in appreciation of Mr. Miyamura's service more than half a
century earlier in the hills and fields of Bruyères two oceans and
a lifetime away.

Mrs. Miyamura continued gazing at the flag in her lap.
Penelope's daughter Keala kept her head down, staring fiercely
at the tops of her black shoes. Penelope's ex-husband Randall
had put in a brief appearance but left early. Typical, Penelope
thought, but then felt guilty for such an uncharitable reaction.
He had never even attended a funeral before he married
Penelope and had to deal with her family and friends. Penelope
knew how hard it was for him to deal with the concrete reality
of death, so she appreciated what an effort it must have been for
him to come.

Penelope's thoughts wandered back to the guessing game

she had played with her father when he'd take her to Scotty's Drive-In on Saturday nights when she was in elementary school. "Do you see what I see?" he would say as they waited in the parking lot. "I see something white," he might say. He always started with a color.

"Is it in the car?" she'd ask.

"No."

She'd scan the parking lot. "Is it bigger than our car?"

"Not really."

She saw someone with a vanilla ice cream cone. "Can I eat it?"

"Nope."

"Is it close to the car?"

"Yes."

She'd look at everything white near the car. "Is it part of a tire?"

"No."

"Is it a piece of paper, is it the paper cup over there, is it part of the building?"

"Nope."

The parking lot was full of white objects—a napkin, a straw wrapper, the streetlight, the lines to mark the parking stalls.

"The white line on the ground." Yes yes yes!

What had reminded Penelope of that game? It must have been the young soldier's white gloves, she thought. Penelope tried unsuccessfully not to start crying again but couldn't help it. Dad would have thought she was silly and overly emotional, but she didn't care. The green grass, her daughter, her mother, and the flag in her mother's lap blurred as the tears welled up again.

Two years after the funeral, Keala announced she was joining the National Guard after graduation. "No, you're not,"

Penelope had responded firmly.

"I'll be 18 soon and I can do whatever I want!" Keala had screamed at her. Never in her life had Penelope even considered the possibility that Keala would do something like this. The draft had ended just before Keala's father Randall had graduated from high school, so he never had to serve in Vietnam. Penelope herself had been against the Vietnam War but was a little too young to have participated in the antiwar demonstrations back then. She remembered passing by UH and seeing the tent city in front of Bachman Hall and the weird bamboo structure that some old Japanese guy had constructed as a symbol of peace or something. She remembered her father, a 442nd veteran who got his engineering degree through the GI Bill and worked for the military, had supported the war until he had gone to Saigon during one of his overseas TDY trips. He talked about it only once, and all he said was, "We have no business being there." Penelope's father was the only one in the family who had served in the military, but he had never talked much about World War II, so Penelope had no idea how Keala had gotten the idea of joining the National Guard. What if the government got more involved in Afghanistan, or worse? No, she would not allow Keala to join if she could help it.

Mrs. Miyamura was slicing cucumbers for her namasu when Penelope arrived with the groceries from Times. "Keala's joining so you don't have to pay for college," Mrs. Miyamura said as Penelope opened the refrigerator to put away the tofu, orange juice, eggs, and tomatoes.

"She doesn't have to pay for college," Penelope replied. "Randall says he'll pay for her college tuition. She knows that."

"You think she'll let him?" Mrs. Miyamura snapped. "She's just like you. So hard head. You think she doesn't know you ripped up all those checks Randall tried to give you to help pay for the house after you divorced him?"

"I let him help pay for her expenses. I just didn't want him to pay for my house. I wanted to take care of myself. I always let him help out with Keala."

"Hard head just like your father. I saw how you struggled trying to get by on your teacher's salary. Bus drivers make more money than you do. You could have been anything—a doctor, a lawyer—but you have no common sense. You could have gotten alimony from that no-good Randall. You supported him through law school when you should have gone yourself. The more educated a person is, the less common sense they have. You're book smart but so stupid!"

"Zip it, Mom. You always say the same thing. You keep rehashing the same old stuff. No wonder Dad got so mad at you sometimes." Penelope shut the refrigerator door firmly.

Mrs. Miyamura looked hurt. "Dad was such a pleasant man. He never complained and he never got angry."

Penelope looked at her mother incredulously. What planet had her mother moved to since Dad died?

Mrs. Miyamura started chopping iceberg lettuce for a salad. She was using more force than necessary. "You should have given Keala a real girl's name, instead of Keala. How come you gave her a boy's name?"

"Mom! Keala can be a girl's name too. There's lots of names that can be either a girl name or a boy name—Jamie, Stacy, Morgan, Robin, Cory, Jan, Dana, Kelly, Courtney, Drew—lots of names."

"If you gave her a real girl's name she wouldn't join the National Guard. She wouldn't surf like a boy either."

"I can't talk to you. You're . . . hopeless!" The cans of chicken broth that Penelope had been stacking fell sideways and rolled onto the counter.

"You the one hard head!" Mrs. Miyamura snapped,

bringing her knife down one more time on the hapless iceberg lettuce.

Penelope and Keala were having dinner at Columbia Inn. They both ordered the fried saimin with teri chicken.

"Keala," Penelope said, "I can help pay your college tuition. So can your father. We want to pay for your college. We always planned to."

"Mommy, I already decided, so don't even try to change my mind." Keala shot an angry glance at Penelope.

Okay, Penelope thought, she's only going to dig her heels in more if I try to talk her out of this but I have to try. "You read the news, don't you, Keala? Bush is going to do something horrible—look at what's happening in Afghanistan! Wars nowadays are fought over money and oil, not about ideals like freedom and democracy. Do you think the government cares about you? Look at what happened to those Desert Storm veterans who had those mysterious illnesses. Look at how the government denied them medical benefits and treated them so horribly because they couldn't prove what their illnesses were caused by. Obviously there was something they were exposed to during the Gulf War that made them sick. It's disgusting that those veterans couldn't get decent medical care."

"Jesus, Mommy. You're such a hippie."

"I am not a hippie." Penelope's voice was starting to rise a little. "Hippies were apolitical. They didn't care about politics or what was really happening in the world. I was never a flower child type. Don't call me a hippie."

"Whatever. Anyway, it's not like I'm joining the Army or anything. It's the National Guard—I can serve here and go to school at the same time."

"Keala, you don't know that for sure. What if they send you away? What if you get deployed?"

"That's part of the deal. If I get deployed, I have to go. Usually, they send the reservists and other people before they send the Guard. Don't worry so much. You always think of the worst that could happen."

"That's because I know more than you do," Penelope replied.

"What do you know? Were you ever in a war like Grandpa?"

Penelope was stunned. "Is this what this is about? You think Grandpa would be happy if you joined the National Guard and got college tuition money? You're thinking of how Grandpa went to college on the GI Bill after the war? Grandpa would want you to finish college, not join the National Guard."

"I want to do it all myself. You didn't take money from Daddy for the house. How come? He would have given it to you."

"That's different. We're not talking about that—we're talking about this fucking crazy idea you have about joining the National Guard."

"Mommy! Don't swear!"

"You listen to me, young lady, you are going to apply to a mainland college, and your father and I will pay for it. You can't join the National Guard. I won't allow it."

"There's nothing you can do about it," Keala replied as their fried saimin and teri chicken plates arrived. Penelope knew Keala was right; there wasn't anything she could do about it. What could she do? Kick Keala out of the house? No, there was nothing she could do about it.

The next year seemed to go too fast for Penelope. Keala joined the National Guard in spite of her father's bribes (a new car and her own apartment, which were both refused) and Penelope's threats ("I'll never talk to you again"). Penelope was appalled at how much like her own mother she was acting, but she just couldn't help herself. Trying to induce guilt didn't work any better on Keala than it had on her either. She had implored, sighed, and cried—"What am I going to do if something happens to you?"—"All I want is for you to have a good life."—"I must have done something wrong to make you want to join the National Guard." Keala registered at Kapi'olani Community College and progressed in her National Guard training. Then the U.S. invaded Iraq and Penelope waited for what she had been afraid of ever since Keala had joined the Guard. Months of dread passed, and Penelope started to hope that maybe Keala would be able to finish her three-year commitment uneventfully. But one night, soon after Penelope started daring to hope that she had been mistaken in her fear, the six o'clock news confirmed she had been miserably right all along—the Hawaii Army National Guard 29th Infantry Brigade—3,100 young men and women, 2,000 of them local— were going to be deployed to Iraq.

Keala was out with her friends, so Penelope waited in the living room, watching the same news stories cycle over and over on CNN. Penelope found some comfort in the story of the cat that had survived for a week trapped in some airplane cargo crate with no food or water. It was a scrawny little thing with huge eyes, and Penelope wished she could hold it. When Penelope heard Keala pull into the garage, she ran to the back door to hug her. "Do you have to go to Iraq? Is your unit one of the ones that have to go?" Penelope started to cry.

"Mommy, it'll be okay. Really." Keala patted her mother's back. "I have to go. Anyway, I won't be assigned to combat duty."

"It doesn't matter if you're not assigned to combat duty; you'll be in combat situations. You'll be in Bush's stupid immoral war. That liar! You could get killed."

"Mommy, I don't think I can talk to you about this. You're hysterical. The other guys will take care of me. You know, the soldier's creed: 'I will always place the mission first. I will never accept defeat. I will never quit. I will never leave a fallen comrade.' The other guys will watch out for me."

"Oh my God, they've brainwashed you!" Penelope released Keala so she could look into her eyes. "They've brainwashed my baby and they're sending her to Iraq." Penelope sobbed and pulled Keala close to her again.

"Jesus, Mommy." Keala let herself be hugged again. "You're so so so . . . nuts."

"I can't help it. Wait until you have a daughter."

"Mommy, let's just try to have a good time until I have to go, okay?"

Penelope looked at Keala. When did her daughter get to be a grown-up, so sure of herself, so seemingly unafraid? It happened almost secretly, like a seed that you don't even know is there that germinates hidden underground, then pushes its way up and pokes its tender shoot above the ground unfolding a little leaf, and before you know it, it's a plant; and then miracle of miracles, a small flower bud emerges from the tip of a stem and blooms like a white star in a green universe. Penelope started to cry again.

"Jesus, Mommy. Stop crying already. It'll be okay."

It was Saturday, and Penelope was picking up her mother to go shopping and dropping off Keala at the beach. Keala's surfboard was strapped to the top of the car. Mrs. Miyamura frowned when she looked at it.

"So Keala, you going surfing today? You don't want to come shopping with us?" Mrs. Miyamura said.

"Grandma, I already told my friends I'm meeting them at the beach," Keala said. "They'll give me a ride home."

"So Keala, you know when you have to go to Iraq?" Mrs. Miyamura asked.

"First we go mainland for training. I think we go to Iraq in February next year."

Penelope's eyes were tearing up again. Mrs. Miyamura looked at her and said, "Better not cry when you're driving. You're going to get us in an accident."

"Do you see what I see?" Keala asked from the back seat. Penelope could see her daughter gazing out toward Diamond Head in her rearview mirror. Keala must have played this game with her grandpa. Mrs. Miyamura was quiet. "I see something white," Keala continued.

"Is it inside the car?" asked Penelope.

"Nope."

"Is it bigger than this car?

"Yes."

"What shape is it?"

"Mommy, you know you have ask a question that I can answer with only 'yes' or 'no.'"

"Okay, is it round?"

"Not really."

"Is it man-made?"

"Nope."

"It's a cloud," Mrs. Miyamura said suddenly, surprising both Keala and Penelope. "The one over there, over Diamond Head."

"Wow, Grandma, you're right. How did you guess?"

"I knew," Mrs. Miyamura said. "Just like I know that Grandpa will watch over you no matter where you are. Because he was a good man, and he wants you to come back to us."

Penelope looked in the rearview mirror at Keala. Penelope had not seen Keala cry at Grandpa Miyamura's funeral, but now Keala's eyes were moist with tears. Keala dabbed her eyes quickly and composed herself. "Ho, Grandma, I never knew you was one psychic!" she tried to joke.

"I know more than you think," Mrs. Miyamura said gravely.

"Mom, you miss Dad, don't you," Penelope said, driving past the zoo and heading for Keala's favorite surf spot.

Mrs. Miyamura nodded. "Sometimes I think he's still here."

"We miss him too," Penelope said softly, "don't we, Keala?" In her rearview mirror, she saw Keala, who appeared to be looking at the sky above Diamond Head, nod in agreement.

Penelope pulled over so Keala could unload her board. Keala leaned toward the front seats and kissed her mother and grandmother. "See you about 7:00," she said. "Maria will bring me home." Keala undid the straps and lifted the surfboard, tucked it under her arm, and headed for her spot.

Penelope looked at her mother, who was watching Keala stride away from the car. "It's going to be okay," Penelope said suddenly, not knowing exactly what she was referring to.

"Of course it's going to be okay," Mrs. Miyamura said, "but not if you sit here going nowhere. If you don't hurry up, we're not going to get a good parking space at Kahala Mall."

"Okay, okay." As Penelope drove down the street, she glanced at her rearview mirror and saw Keala turn down the right-of-way to the beach. Then Penelope looked toward Diamond Head. She could see the white cloud was drifting toward the ocean and wondered how many surfers were out today, bobbing patiently on their boards waiting to catch whatever the ocean offered them, perfectly aware of the rocks and razor sharp reef below the surface between them and the shore. What did they see as they rode that glassy curve of sheer fluid power, propelled by an ocean they couldn't control? Penelope saw a break in the traffic and turned, merging with the other cars traveling beyond the Diamond Head lookout points, all headed for undisclosed destinations.

No Place Like Paradise

THE GIRL IN THE PHOTOGRAPH that fell out of my father's
Bible looked like him, but I didn't know who she was. She had
my father's eyes but was pretty. My father was sort of handsome
when he was young, but not pretty, so it was funny to see the
resemblance. You think you know everything you need to know
about your parents, and then they surprise you after they're
dead. My father had died twenty years ago, but it was a year
after my mother passed away before I was finally able to make
myself clean out their house. That's when I found the photo.
I was surprised that my father had a Bible, since he was not a
religious man—in fact he was a self-declared agnostic and had
told me when I was six years old that he wasn't smart enough to
know for sure that God did not exist, but if God did exist, then
the world would be different—bad people would not get away
with the bad things they did. So when I found the Bible with his
name written on the inside of the front cover, I was surprised,
and when the photo fell out, I knew I had to ask Uncle Buddy
about it.

Buddy Kealoha was not my real uncle; he was my father's
best friend. They had grown up together and each had a tattoo
on the part of his left hand between his thumb and index finger
with the initial for his last name. I remember my father's tattoo,
which looked like two pointed mountains stuck together to
form an *M*, for Miyamura. Uncle Buddy's tattoo looked like
a *V* on a line and was supposed to be a *K*. When I was little, I
begged for a tattoo, so my father used a magic marker to draw
an *N* for Naomi on my hand. My mother scolded us both, and
the tattoo was never redrawn. When I was ten, my father died
in a head-on collision with a drunk driver. Uncle Buddy kept

an eye on my mother and me after that. I always wondered if Uncle Buddy and Mom would ever get together, but they never did. When Mom got cancer and all her hair fell out because of the chemo treatments, Uncle Buddy showed up bolohead—he had shaved his thick curly graying hair off. "How do you like my new hairstyle?" he had said. He made Mom laugh for the first time in months. She gasped when she stopped laughing and replied, "Stylish, but you have to shave off the eyebrows for the total look." He had replied, "Hey, the eyebrows is where I draw the line." And we all laughed till we cried. Two years later she died. Uncle Buddy and I were at her bedside when she took her last breath.

Uncle Buddy didn't answer his phone. It was mullet season, so I knew I might possibly find him somewhere along Diamond Head Beach between the lighthouse and Doris Duke's Shangri-La. I put the photo in a Ziploc and stuck it in my tote bag. I had to talk to Uncle Buddy anyway because I had just gotten promoted out of robberies and assaults and had been assigned my first murder case as a public defender. Uncle Buddy didn't approve of my work—he said most of my clients were probably guilty plus he thought it was dangerous for a woman to associate with criminals. I parked the car on the road and walked down the long asphalt path to the beach. The recent landslide that had covered part of the path had been cleared, but there were warning signs that stated everyone who went down the path was doing so at their own risk. The signs didn't stop anyone—there were just as many surfers and beachgoers walking up and down the path as usual. Unlike Waikīkī Beach, at Diamond Head, most of the crowd was surfing the waves, not sun-tanning on the beach. Far down the beach I could see a few figures standing who might have been throwing net, but there was no way I could tell if one of them was Uncle Buddy. I'd just have to walk all the way over to see.

I finally found Uncle Buddy. He was wearing his UH Rainbows baseball cap and polarized sunglasses, and getting his throw net ready to cast into the water.

"E Naomi, what you doing here?" He smiled. "You came 'cause you feel like going fishing or what? The mullet are running." It seemed like a long time since I had enjoyed the way the waves reflected the sunlight and the sound of the waves breaking near the shore. I greeted him with a kiss on the cheek, local style.

"Yeah, I guess I miss watching you throw net. Seen any mullet yet?"

"Not yet. Gotta wait. I know they stay out there, swimming, playing in the water." Uncle Buddy gazed out at the waves. I was always amazed at how he always seemed to be able to see the mullet in the waves, their torpedo-shaped brown shadows in the face of a wave as it rose up before crashing down.

I didn't want to mess up his fishing, but I really wanted to show him the photo, and it seemed like the right moment since he wasn't fishing yet, and he didn't seem to be in any rush. "Can I ask you something?"

"Shoots. What's up?"

"I found this photo in Dad's Bible," I said, pulling the Ziploc out of my bag. "I thought you might know who it is." Was it my imagination, or did Uncle Buddy flinch? He looked at the photo and his eyes seemed to get a little misty. He opened his mouth slightly as if to speak, hesitated, and then said, "I didn't know your father still had any pictures of her. She's your Auntie Pearl. Your father's half-sister. She disappeared before you were born."

All I could hear was the roaring of the ocean. Why did the light seem suddenly so bright? "Dad had a half-sister?" I was stunned. Uncle Buddy didn't answer. I went on, "What do you mean, she disappeared? Did she run away? Was she kidnapped? What happened to her? Why didn't Mom and Dad ever say anything about her?" The questions tumbled out.

Uncle Buddy busied himself with his net, draping its gathered bulk over his left arm and using his right hand to arrange the net's lead-weighted edges so the net would blossom into a graceful wide circle in the air before it sank down on its prey. He didn't look at me. He just started talking about fishing. "When you go fishing for mullet, you gotta be patient. You gotta wait for da the right moment to throw your net. Mullet are smart. They know you're waiting for them, so they spook easy. And if you throw even half a second too early or too late, you miss 'em—you get all kinds of other fish you no like or you no can eat. Some people like manini, but I no like waste time with manini—too small."

Why was he talking about fishing now? Why wasn't he answering my questions about the girl in the photograph? Uncle Buddy continued, "Watch out if you try throwing net from the reef. Don't throw where your net can get stuck. Watch your step 'cause there's eels in the rocks. Ho, eels is ugly buggahs. Mean. Once they bite you, it's aloha to whatever part they bit, bruddah. All kinds of danger in the ocean." Then he added, "Danger in paradise." Sometimes Uncle Buddy was so dramatic.

I didn't want to force the issue; after all he was my uncle and I was supposed to show him respect and wait for him to get to the answer, but I couldn't help myself. I blurted out, "Uncle, what do you mean 'she disappeared?'"

"Your auntie just nevah come home one night. They found her car by at the Pali Lookout. People suspected her boyfriend. He was one mean bastard—we couldn't figure out how come she ever went hook up with him or how come she stayed with him. Police never found anything. So people said maybe was one double suicide—maybe the boyfriend went kill her and then killed himself. Plenny people commit suicide up there on the Pali. Or maybe the boyfriend went kill her and flew to the mainland to disappear. Or maybe she eloped with that pilau dirty bastard because we all hated him so much. Fucking asshole shithead kūkae bastard." Uncle Buddy piled on the swear words when he got mad. Uncle Buddy looked at me, narrowing his eyes the way he did whenever he wanted me to pay attention to what he was saying.

"Naomi, no waste time fishing where you only going catch rubbish fish. Or worse."

"Uncle, how come my parents never said anything about Auntie Pearl?" It felt funny to say the name of this auntie I had never known about.

Uncle Buddy gazed out toward the horizon. "Your Auntie Pearl was a good person—kind to everyone, pretty, sweet. Really nahenahe—you know, really gentle. It broke your father's heart when she disappeared. That was before he met your mother. Your mother made him happy again."

I needed to know what happened to Auntie Pearl. "Was her last name Miyamura, same as mine?"

"Hey, don't you start getting ideas about digging up stuff. No, she had different last name; she was a widow already when she met that no good shit boyfriend. I forget her last name— Cambra, Cabrillo, Castillo, something like that, or maybe it started with a *B* or something."

I couldn't believe how badly Uncle Buddy lied. I didn't know anyone who had a sharper memory for names and faces than he did. Of course he knew her last name—he just didn't want to tell me. But a little research should be all it took. I was confident.

"I can feel the mullet calling me," he said. "I going in." Uncle Buddy waded into the water carefully, up to his waist.

The waves rose in glassy walls in front of him. I could see him scanning the waves, looking for those brown shadows. Suddenly he swung his arms back and threw his net in a wide arc toward the waves. The net opened into a circle and seemed to be momentarily suspended in the air before it touched the water and sank instantly under the surface. He splashed toward his net and started picking it up. He waded back toward the shore, the net heavy with fish. I ran toward the shore break to help him. I loved watching Uncle Buddy throw net, but I hated pulling the fish from the net. I had to do it, though, because otherwise he'd make fun of me. Plus it would be rude not to help him. Uncle Buddy threw the first mullet back into the ocean as a thank-you to the fishing gods. I tried to keep my face from screwing up as I worked to extricate the fish that were too small to keep. I had to get them out of the net before they died so I could throw them back in the water. Their mouths gasped desperately sucking in the deadly air, so I had to work fast. Uncle Buddy was happily pulling the mullet from the net and throwing them into his cooler. "Woohoo! I can taste that Chinese parsley, shoyu, ginger, and hot oil sizzling on the steamed mullet already. Ho, my mouth is watering already!" I was having a hard time controlling my face as I tried to pull each undersized slippery cold slimy fish from the net. In spite of all my efforts, Uncle Buddy started laughing at me.

"Use your whole hand to grab—don't just pick with your fingers like you at one tea party at the Moana Hotel. And stop looking so scared of the fish. You such a princess."

He knew how to get me—I hated it when he called me a princess —it was an insult.

"I got my first murder case," I said, trying to act more macho with the fish.

"Be careful. You don't know who you might be defending. You nevah know who might get pissed off at you for defending the guy," he said as he threw the last mullet into his cooler. He looked at me, narrowing his eyes again. "And don't get any ideas about investigating on your own. The Public Defenders office get its own investigators. You let 'em do their job."

"Yeah yeah," I said, pretending to humor him.

"I know you. You hard head, just like your father and mother," he replied. "At least take a self-defense class unless you get one boyfriend you nevah tell me about yet who can take care you."

That wasn't a bad idea, taking a self-defense class.

I had no luck trying to find out much about Auntie Pearl. Actually, I had to get started on my first murder case, so I had to put Auntie Pearl on the back burner for a while. I met my client in jail. He had gotten into a fight outside a Korean bar and the guy he was fighting with fell backwards, hit his head on the pavement, and died of massive head injuries.

My client walked into the visiting area with his head down. He was in his early 20s, medium height, tan, with a surfer's wide shoulders and narrow hips. He wasn't the usual middle-aged Asian guy who I thought comprised the typical Korean bar clientele. He didn't look like a killer either.

"Hello, Mr. Park. I'm your attorney, Naomi Miyamura."

"So I got a girl attorney," he said glumly. "Just call me Sean. You want me to call you Ms. Miyamura?"

"Whatever you're comfortable with, Sean."

"Okay, Ms. Miyamura, what do you want to know that isn't already in the police report?"

Sean Park had attitude, which might be a problem in court. I could see I would have to work on him. I better not tell him this was my first murder case. Not yet. "Just tell me what happened, in your own words."

He didn't exactly look remorseful or scared—he just

looked depressed. So I asked him again. "What happened?"

He looked at his hands. "The guy insulted my sister. So I called him on it, told him to apologize or at least leave her alone. And we got into it. The bouncers threw us guys out. He saw me in the parking lot and attacked me. He pushed me so I pushed back. I guess he sort of tripped on a bump or pothole in the parking lot. It wasn't my fault. He started it."

"Did your sister know him very well?"

"I don't think so. He wasn't one of her regulars."

"Your sister still working in the bar?"

"No. They fired her after the guy died. She's working at Seoul Moon Restaurant, that Korean restaurant on Keʻeaumoku Street, the one that's open all night. No bar wants to hire her now because of what happened."

Sean must have immigrated when he was young—he didn't have much of an accent and sounded like he was local. I couldn't figure why his sister would be working at a Korean bar. Maybe she was older than he was and never overcame the language barrier. Sean didn't have much more to say, so I figured I'd just talk more to him next time. I made a mental note to find the sister and visit the scene of the crime.

The self-defense class was a two-day weekend session, which was fine with me. The instructor, Sam Talman, was part Samoan, but just looked hapa—mixed like a lot of people in Hawaiʻi, part haole, Caucasian, that is, and part something else. He wasn't young, but he was in prime condition and obviously spent time at the gym. Of course after he put on all that padding, he looked more like the Michelin Man than a buffed out older athlete, but he had nice eyes. I wondered how many of his students, who appeared to be mostly professional type women in their 30s and 40s, had little crushes on him.

One rather elegant looking woman in her 40s raised her

hand and asked, "Are you going to teach us how to kick a guy in the balls?" Talk about having no shame—her question was embarrassing, so everyone laughed.

Sam Talman smiled wearily and said, "I'll show you how to kick a guy in the balls, but I'm also going to show you way better ways to foil an attacker. Why is it that so many women think that kicking a guy in the nuts is the best defense? What if your aim is not so great? You could get in even worse trouble. There are other more effective ways to defend yourself." He looked at each student in the class to make sure he was making his point impressively enough. "So let's get started."

He proceeded to show us how to deter an attacker by using the heel of a hand and pushing up into the attacker's nose, stomping on the instep of an attacker's foot, using our elbows and arms to escape from an attacker's hold, and swinging a bag like a club. The point was to disable the attacker long enough to run away and get help. The point was to scream bloody murder, escape, and run like hell. Then he made us practice our self-defense skills on him. Most of us were a little inhibited so he had to resort to some yelling to encourage us to act as if we were really being attacked. When it was my turn, I didn't do it right the first time.

"Just because you're petite doesn't mean you can't do some damage," Sam Talman told me. "You look strong, don't be afraid to grind your heel down; don't be afraid to push hard, straight up into the guy's nose. You can do it. And you have to scream. Come on—SCREAM!"

I didn't tell him that my recurring nightmare was that I could never scream when I was in danger—only a thin airy high-pitched sound came out from my constricted throat in my nightmares. So I dug my heel into his foot as hard as I could, elbowed his ribs with such force that he grunted, shoved the palm of my hand into his nose guard with a vengeance, and ran away as fast as I could. But I couldn't scream. And I could produce only a weak "AAAAaaa" in class.

So I said, "I think I just need to practice the scream more."

Maybe my best self-defense would be just to outrun my attacker. In spite of my paltry vocal performance, I still got a certificate for completing the class, so I stuck it low on the wall in my office in the corner behind my desk where almost no one could see it.

I was looking at the crime scene photos and the police report when Jake Alvarez, the investigator assigned to my case, poked his head in my doorway.

"Hey," Jake said, "What do you want me to do?"

"Hi Jake. We gotta talk to the sister and interview some witnesses at the bar." I pointed to the photo of the victim on my desk. "He's old enough to be my father—how old is Sean Park's sister? Know anything about the victim?"

"He's probably underworld," said Jake. "No known employment. Originally from here, but moved to the mainland a while ago. Looks like he was visiting from Oakland."

Jake was old enough to maybe remember my Auntie Pearl's disappearance, so I said as casually as I could, "Hey Jake, you remember some case about a girl who disappeared from her car at the Pali Lookout maybe a little over thirty years ago? Unsolved case?"

"Oh yeah," Jake said, "the boyfriend was the main suspect, but he disappeared too. Never found any bodies. The boyfriend had underworld connections. He was a no-good bastard. What was his name? Newman? Nogales? Norman?" Jake frowned, looking down at my desk. Then he looked at me, his eyes widened in that aha-moment look he always got when he had just figured something out. "Noland. Sonofagun! I think the victim in your case has the same last name as that girl's boyfriend. Noland. Wonder if they're related."

"You remember the girl's name?"

"Yeah. Leimomi Kam."

I was disappointed her name wasn't Pearl. Then Jake said, "Her name was Leimomi, but the family and friends called her another name—some kind of jewel, something like Pearl or Opal."

The crime scene was the parking lot of Club Clarice, one of dozens of Korean bars in the Ala Moana area. Jake and I looked at the police report and pinpointed the place that the victim hit his head. It was near the last stall next to the back door of the club, not far from the parking lot exit. The asphalt looked pretty smooth—I couldn't see any potholes or bumps that the victim, Alvin G. Noland, could have tripped over.

"Jake, Sean said Alvin Noland must have stepped into a pothole and fallen. Did they resurface this parking lot?"

"This parking lot was always pretty well maintained," Jake replied, looking at the two cars parked near the entrance of the club. "Noland maybe had too much to drink. Plus he was in his 60s—maybe couldn't hold his liquor so good any more, maybe reflexes not working so good any more. A push from a strong young guy could make him fall straight backwards and hit his head."

The bar was closed, so I'd have to come back at night to interview the possible witnesses. When I got home, there was a message on my answering machine from Uncle Buddy.

"Naomi, I saw an article in the newspaper about your case. I gotta talk to you. Call me."

Uncle Buddy had probably seen the victim's name. I dialed his number and he picked up immediately. "Naomi, try get yourself off the case. The Nolands are underworld. Your guy is dead already. You don't want no trouble."

"Uncle, it's my first case. I can't ask to be reassigned. It's my job."

"You find anything out about your Auntie Pearl's case?" Uncle Buddy sounded like he was trying to sound nonchalant.

"Not really. I have to work on my client's case first." I couldn't resist adding, "I did find out her last name, though. Kam. And that her given name was Leimomi, not Pearl." I didn't tell him that Jake had told me that the victim in my case and Auntie Pearl's boyfriend had the same last name.

"Oh yeah, I forgot her legal name was Leimomi. 'Momi' means 'pearl'—that's how she got the name Pearl." I knew Uncle Buddy was just pretending he had forgotten Pearl's legal name. Then he asked, "The guy your client killed—did he have another name? You know how plenny people get one legal name and then another name the family calls them? Like your Auntie Pearl's name was Leimomi, but no one called her that."

"Not that we know of."

Uncle Buddy lowered his voice. "Naomi, don't go anywhere alone—let me know if you gotta go someplace at night and I'll come with you."

Uncle Buddy was starting to freak me out but I had to act like he wasn't scaring me. What did he know about the Nolands that he wasn't telling me? Why didn't he tell me that Noland was the last name of Auntie Pearl's boyfriend? "Uncle, no worry. I'll be fine. Nothing's going to happen."

I should have listened to my Uncle Buddy about being more cautious. A week later I met some friends for dinner downtown. I had parked my car in the Harbor Square parking structure instead of on the street. Dinner went on longer than I thought it would, and like a fool, I told my friends that I didn't need to be walked to my car. The parking structure was a little creepy even in the daytime because the ceilings were low and the lighting was so bad. There were all kinds of hidden corners, and the parking lot seemed to be designed to disorient people. I gripped my keys tightly in my fist as I exited the elevator, trying to locate the area I had parked my car so I could make a beeline for it. I was a couple columns away from my car when out of the corner of my eye, I saw something move. Then I heard footsteps. My throat felt dry and I started to run toward my car. Someone was running after me but I was too scared to look. Footsteps pounded closer. Someone grabbed my arm, pulled me back, and wrapped his arms around my upper arms and chest. His hands were large and thick, and I saw a tattoo of a Z at the base of his stubby left thumb. I thrust my right elbow back to twist out of his hold and dug my heel into his instep with all the force I could muster. His hold loosened. I catapulted away from him and ran toward my car, still gripping my keys in my fist. I beeped my car door open, jumped in, slammed the door shut, hit the automatic lock, and started pounding the horn with my left hand as I tried to slide the key into the ignition with my right hand. All I saw was his back as he limped toward the elevator and stairwell—he was maybe a little under six feet tall and heavyset, wearing a black hoodie and long pants. Just like in my nightmares, I hadn't screamed, but my throat felt tight and raw as if I had.

"Did you see your attacker's face at all?" Officer Jeremiah Chun asked. His classic Chinese-Hawaiian good looks were a little disconcerting. He was too handsome for his own good, but he wasn't my type. At least that's what I tried to tell myself as I looked at the golden brown flecks in his hazel eyes; his irises looked like olivines touched with golden light. He said something as the wail of ambulance sirens passed by Ala Moana Boulevard below us. I didn't quite catch what he said, so he had to repeat himself. "Any unusual marks?"

I described the Z tattoo at the base of the attacker's thumb, pointing at the corresponding area of my left hand. Two other officers were looking around the parking lot and the elevator. I heard footsteps behind me and turned to see Uncle Buddy walking toward us from the ramp. I had called him after calling 911, and he had driven down even though I had told him not to. He was visibly agitated and out of breath. "Naomi! Didn't I tell you be careful? Those guys are dangerous."

Jeremiah Chun did a double-take. "Is this your dad? What guys is he talking about? Do you know who might have tried to attack you?"

"This is my Uncle Buddy. There's no one out to get me. It was just a random attack. I was just in the wrong place at the wrong time."

"No, it's not just random," Uncle Buddy said. He was getting into his insistent pa'akikī mode, which meant soon he would be so hard head, it would be impossible to argue with him. "Somebody wants you off the case."

Jeremiah Chun suddenly looked more interested. "What case?" He turned to me. "You one attorney?"

"Yes. But this has nothing to do with my case. My client is accused of murder, but it was an accident."

Uncle Buddy's voice was getting louder. "You don't know if it had nothing to with your case. I been telling you, the guy your client killed got connections to the underworld. The attack is connected to your case. I can feel it."

Now Jeremiah Chun was definitely interested. "Who did your client kill?"

"He's accused of murder. Innocent until proven guilty, remember?" I was getting irritated by this whole conversation.

"That's just attorney bullshit," Uncle Buddy muttered. "The guy her client killed was a Noland."

Jeremiah Chun didn't seem impressed.

Uncle Buddy looked first at Officer Chun, then at me. "The Nolands are related to Lucania."

Duke Lucania was one of the reputed local godfather types from the 1970s, but I hadn't heard anything about him in years. Everyone said Lucania wasn't his real name, but no one knew who his real parents were. I thought he was dead. No wonder Uncle Buddy thought Auntie Pearl's boyfriend was bad news.

Jeremiah Chun had stopped scribbling on his notepad. "Lucania is semi-retired, staying under the radar. The younger generation too crazy—too much ice and crack. And why would Lucania go after her?" he said. "Why not go after the client who's in jail?"

"I dunno why. But I can feel it," Uncle Buddy said. He turned his attention back to me. "What's the matter with your friends? Letting you go back to your car by yourself downtown late at night. What kind friends you get? No mo' gentlemen or what?"

"Uncle, they offered to walk me to my car, but I didn't want to impose on them. I never had trouble before."

"Even if you refused, good guys would walk you anyway. Their parents never raise them right, fuckin' inconsiderate assholes. They all attorneys or what?"

"Uncle. Was my fault. I told them I thought it was perfectly fine."

"Good thing you took that self-defense class. Look, your arm is bruised."

"So that's how you knew how to get away," Jeremiah Chun said. "Who'd you take the class from?"

"Sam Talman."

"He's good. He really knows his stuff. He was an investigative reporter before. He learned his stuff on the job—I heard stories about him from my dad. He was hardcore. No more reporters like him anymore. Too bad." Jeremiah looked at his notepad. "Black hoodie, Z tattoo, walks with a limp probably because of what you did to his foot. Won't be limping for long."

"Z tattoo? Around here?" Uncle Buddy touched the K tattoo at the base of his thumb. I nodded. Uncle Buddy said firmly, "Wasn't a Z. Was one N." Then I remembered that fake tattoo my dad had drawn on my hand. If I turned my hand a certain way, it looked like a Z. Was Uncle Buddy right?

Jeremiah Chun made a note. "The tattoo, Z or N, is good info. We'll look for prints and anything else around here." He closed his notepad.

"I guess that's all. Call me if you remember anything else." He handed me his card.

Cops are the enemy, I thought to myself, but I couldn't help wishing I could remember something else so I could call Jeremiah Chun of the olivine gold-flecked eyes, even though he really wasn't my type.

"I'll follow you home," Uncle Buddy said, "so I can make sure you're safe. You drive me to my car and I'll follow you."

I have to admit it was comforting to see Uncle Buddy's silver Corolla behind me as I drove home to Kaimukī. It was drizzling and traffic was light. Uncle Buddy walked me up to the apartment. I was shocked when he calmly pulled out a Smith & Wesson pistol and went from room to room in my small apartment like a cop in the movies, checking every possible hiding place including all the closets, the bathroom, under the kitchen sink, and the lanai. In an odd way, his paranoia was comforting, though the gun made me nervous.

"So you think the tattoo was N for Noland?" I asked.

"Maybe. But if the Nolands really wanted to hurt you, they would have. The guy wanted you to see his tattoo. Either that or he's one amateur." Uncle Buddy didn't give me any credit for using what I had learned in Sam Talman's class. "You sure your client's victim nevah have another name?" he asked again.

"Why do you keep asking about another name?"

"Because your Auntie Pearl's boyfriend was a Noland. But his name wasn't Alvin. At least no one ever called him that. His name was Keoki."

Then it hit me. "Alvin Noland's middle name was George." Keoki is the Hawaiian name for George.

Uncle Buddy slammed his fist on the counter. "I'll never find out what happened to Pearl now! I knew that pilau bastard would come back here someday. I thought I'd get the truth from him when he came back, but now it's too late." He stared at the gun on the counter. I wondered when he had gotten that gun, whether he had gotten it sometime after the police stopped looking for Auntie Pearl, whether he had ever used it. Uncle Buddy had been waiting all these years for Keoki Noland to show up again, hoping to catch him in his net. He had been right that Keoki would return home, but he hadn't foreseen that Keoki would wind up dead only a couple days after coming back.

"Maybe it's not too late," I said.

"Too late," Uncle Buddy said. He sounded so sad.

I never thought about what my parents and Uncle Buddy were like when they were young, before I was born. I knew nothing of the secret they kept from me about Auntie Pearl. Could Uncle Buddy be right that my assailant in the parking lot was connected to my case? I didn't really know what was under the surface of the water, and I needed Uncle Buddy to tell me. He had said there was danger in paradise, and I had to find out what he was really referring to. You think you know everything you need to know about your family, and then they surprise you. It wasn't too late yet for Uncle Buddy and me.

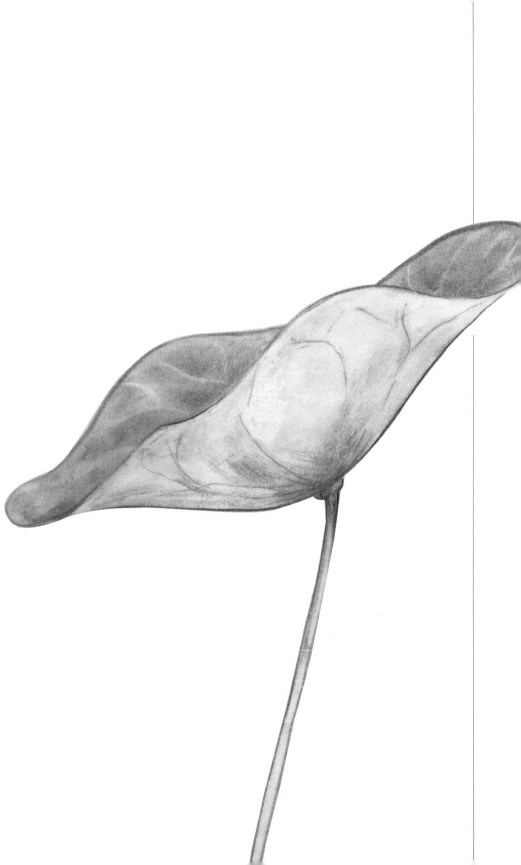

Acknowledgements

I would like to thank the people whose aloha and support helped this book become a reality.

I would like to thank Darrell Lum and Eric Chock for their vision and extraordinary dedication to local literature all these years. I would like to thank Joy Kobayashi-Cintrón and Wing Tek Lum for everything they do to take care of both business and people.

I would to thank President Marie Hara and the other members of the Bamboo Ridge Board of Directors, the State Foundation on Culture and the Arts, and the National Endowment for the Arts for their support.

I would like to thank Normie Salvador and Michael Little for their attention to detail, Hal Lum and Masayo Suzuki for the author photo, and Stephanie Chang for her graphic design.

I am forever indebted to Scott Turow, Sylvia Watanabe, Mindy Pennybacker, and Lois-Ann Yamanaka for their comments about my book.

I am forever grateful to Noe Tanigawa for her art and for all projects we have enjoyed together.

I would like to thank Eduoard Canonica, Pierre Moulin, Chantal and Jean-Pierre Kaspar, André Freminet, Michelle Claudel, adjutant mayor Jean Michaud, and Épinal Cemetery Superintendent Tom Cavaness for making my visit to Bruyères and the Vosges so memorable.

I would like to thank Robert Pennybacker for using my poem

"Journeys to the Horizon" for the documentary *Living Your Dying* and for collaborating with Noe Tanigawa and me on the video project for which "Painted Passages" was written.

I would like to thank Study Group for their critiques and camaraderie. I would like to thank Lisa Kanae, Mavis Hara, and Electa Sam for their support and encouragement. I would like to thank Patricia N. Mahony, who traveled with me to Bruyères, for helping me take care of some final book details and whose friendship continues to transcend both time and distance.

I am grateful for my parents, Saburo and Violet T. Harada, and for my brother, Wesley S. Harada, beyond what words can express.

I am grateful for this place, Hawai'i, the source of stories and inspiration for so many.

Mahalo nui and fondest aloha to all.

About the Author

Gail N. Harada was born in Honolulu and spent part of her childhood on a U.S. Army base in Japan. She has a B.A. from Stanford University and an M.F.A. in English (Creative Writing) from the University of Iowa Writers' Workshop. In 2000, she won a Pushcart Prize for her poem "A Meditation." Her work has been published in *Hawai'i Review*, in regular issues of *Bamboo Ridge*, and in the following anthologies: *The 2000 Pushcart Prize XXIV*, *Breaking Silence: An Anthology of Contemporary Asian American Poets*, *Talk Story: An Anthology of Hawai'i's Local Writers*, *Wahine O Hawai'i*, and *Island Fire: An Anthology of Literature from Hawai'i*. She has written poems for film and art projects. "Painted Passages" was part of a video collaboration with noted Hawai'i artist Noe Tanigawa and filmmaker Robert Pennybacker. "Journeys to the Horizon" was written for *Living Your Dying*, a 2003 documentary about Reverend Mitsuo Aoki and his work with terminal cancer patients. She did a mixed media piece juxtaposing her poem "A Question" with medical bills and chemotherapy records alongside accounts of recent Iraq war dead for the 2006 Koa Gallery exhibit *Witnessing*. She has taught students of all ages and was a Poet in the Schools for several years. She is currently a professor at Kapi'olani Community College, where she teaches writing and literature.

Photos by Gail N. Harada